Trifles

a

Quarterly for Devotees

of

Sherlock Holmes

Volume I

Issue 1

Editor: Darlene A. Cypser

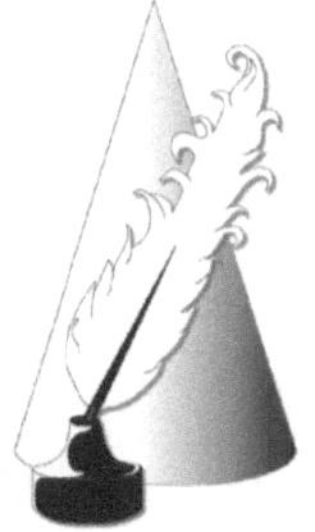

Foolscap & Quill

In addition to the new material, excerpts and images from these public domain works and others were used in this publication: *Windsor Magazine*, *Puck Magazine, The Strand Magazine*, *London's Underground, The Illustrated Police News*.

No AI software was used in the production of this publication or its contents.

ISBN 978-1-938143-68-7

Foolscap & Quill
P.O. Box 1018
Morrison, CO 80465 USA
http://www.foolscap-quill.com

Table of Contents

Illustrations

Trifles

Introduction

"You know my method. It is founded upon the observation of trifles," Sherlock Holmes, "The Boscombe Valley Mystery"

Trifles is intended to bridge the gap between the publications of the various Sherlockian 'scholarly' publications, including those published by Sherlockian societies around the world and the commercial periodicals which also are aimed to appeal to followers of the Master Detective. It is modeled after the periodicals of the late 19th century which contained a variety of stories and articles to satisfy readers of different interests. *Trifles* will include stories, games, puzzles, and artwork, as well as articles of a historical, literary, scientific, or technical nature related to Sherlock Holmes and Dr. John H. Watson. Some articles will be especially interesting to those who are new followers of Sherlock Holmes. Some will be more interesting to those who have been treading in Holmes' footsteps for decades.

The fifty-six short stories and four novellas written about Sherlock Holmes and Dr. Watson are referred to as the Canon. Many Sherlockians use four letter abbreviations for the stories of the Canon in their writing. These abbreviations follow this introduction.

Many Sherlockians play "THE GAME." This means they accept Sherlock Holmes and Dr. John H. Watson as real people and (most of) the adventures recorded in the Canon as events that really occurred. One branch of The Game is the attempt to determine the order in which the cases in the Canon occurred. This is complicated by the fact that Watson may have changed names, dates, and places in converting the cases into, as Holmes put it, "a series of tales." Chronologists take this a step further in attempting to place the date and time that the various adventures took place. While this issue does not contain any essays here regarding chronology, we do have a very useful piece explaining Baker Street finances and how to compare the value of British currency of the 19th century to U.S. dollars today

In this issue of *Trifles* we also have a poem about Dr. Watson's drinking habits, a trivia quiz based on "The Five Orange Pips," a new pastiche, an essay about one person's journey from a casual interest in Sherlock Holmes to being Staff Surgeon of a scion of the Baker Street Irregulars. One essay talks about Lestrade's bulldogishness and another essay tells us about Moriarty's appearance in Batman's universe. Another takes us through the laws related to marriage and other family matters which would have applied to Holmes' cases. These are followed by a crossword puzzle and an article about real 19th century detectives. A chapter about the conditions in London lodging-houses frequented by the poor from Thomas Holmes' book, *London's Underworld*, also appears.

I had not intended to include any of my own writing in this issue. However, only one pastiche was submitted, so I added an excerpt from Chapter Seven of *The Consulting Detective Trilogy Part III: Montague Street*, which is a story about a case taken up by the young Sherlock Holmes on his own initiative during the "long wait" early in his career before he met Dr. Watson.

— DC

Abbreviations for the Sherlock Holmes Canon

These abbreviations were originally proposed by Jay Finley Christ in his *Irregular Guide to Sherlock Holmes of Baker Street* published in 1947. The stories and their abbreviations are listed below in the order they were first published.

STORY TITLE	ABBREVIATION
A Study in Scarlet	STUD
The Sign of the Four	SIGN
A Scandal in Bohemia	SCAN
A Case of Identity	IDEN
The Red-Headed League	REDH
The Boscombe Valley Mystery	BOSC
The Five Orange Pips	FIVE
The Man With the Twisted Lip	TWIS
The Blue Carbuncle	BLUE
The Speckled Band	SPEC
The Engineer's Thumb	ENGR
The Noble Bachelor	NOBL
The Beryl Coronet	BERY
The Copper Beeches	COPP
Silver Blaze	SILV
The Cardboard Box	CARD
The Yellow Face	YELL
The Stock-Broker's Clerk	STOC
The "Gloria Scott"	GLOR
The Musgrave Ritual	MUSG
The Reigate Squires	REIG
The Crooked Man	CROO
The Resident Patient	RESI
The Greek Interpreter	GREE
The Naval Treaty	NAVA
The Final Problem	FINA

The Hound of the Baskervilles	HOUN
The Empty House	EMPT
The Norwood Builder	NORW
The Solitary Cyclist	SOLI
The Dancing Men	DANC
The Priory School	PRIO
The Adventure of Black Peter	BLAC
Charles Augustus Milverton	CHAS
The Six Napoleons	SIXN
The Three Students	3STU
The Golden Pince-Nez	GOLD
The Missing Three-Quarter	MISS
The Abbey Grange	ABBE
The Second Stain	SECO
Wisteria Lodge	WIST
The Bruce-Partington Plans	BRUC
The Devil's Foot	DEVI
The Red Circle	REDC
The Disappearance of Lady Frances Carfax	LADY
The Dying Detective	DYIN
The Valley of Fear	VALL
His Last Bow	LAST
The Adventure of the Mazarin Stone	MAZA
The Problem of Thor Bridge	THOR
The Adventure of the Creeping Man	CREE
The Adventure of the Sussex Vampire	SUSS
The Adventure of the Three Garridebs	3GAR
The Adventure of the Illustrious Client	ILLU
The Adventure of the Blanched Soldier	BLAN
The Adventure of the Retired Colourman	RETI
The Adventure of the Veiled Lodger	VEIL
The Adventure of the Three Gables	3GAB
The Adventure of the Lion's Mane	LION
The Adventure of Shoscombe Old Place	SHOS

The Musings of a Novice Sherlockian

by

Jeff Fladung

"Where did you first learn of Sherlock Holmes?" That is a question I hear repeated on each episode of the "I hear of Sherlock Everywhere," (IHOSE) podcast I listen to now that I have become a Sherlockian. It is interesting to hear the stories of each person interviewed and how they were first introduced to the character of Sherlock Holmes. Each time I hear that question, I try to remember how did I first hear of the great consulting detective and his enduring friend and chronicler, Doctor Watson?

To be truthful, I cannot remember! I do remember reading those anticipated childhood books that came in the Scholastic orders at school such as *The Adventures of the Black Hand Gang*, where you read the story and found clues hidden in a series of drawings.

One series, which could be considered an introduction to Sherlock Holmes for younger kids was Encyclopedia Brown. I loved that series. I tried to find the solution while reading the story. Most of the time I was unsuccessful. Thankfully the solutions were in the back of the book.

Once I got into my teens, I, like most teenagers interested in crime stories, started to read the Hardy Boys books. I read most of them, but not all, as I easily got bored with most of the stories. However, one of the books captured my attention and I read it from cover-to-cover multiple times and referenced the sections throughout the

book depending on what I was interested in. That book was *The Hardy Boys Detective Handbook.* I still have that copy in my bookcase. My favorite chapter is "No Two of Them Alike." The chapter on fingerprints, which I still find fascinating to this day. That's probably why I am the Fingerprint Merit Badge counselor for my son's Scout troop.

During the late 1970s and early 1980s, TV was somewhat limited compared to today. I do remember watching old black and white movies of various sorts but the ones that stand out to me as most memorable were Sherlock Holmes movies played on Saturdays or Sundays, with the main characters portrayed by Basil Rathbone and Nigel Bruce. I remember watching and wondering how Sherlock Holmes was able to figure out who did it or what happened. Then when he explained everything to Doctor Watson it all seemed so obvious, and I could not figure out why it was not obvious to me at the time.

Quite a few years went by after that when I cannot remember if Sherlock Holmes and I crossed paths. I do know that sometime after I graduated high school and joined the Air Force, at my second duty assignment, at Cheyenne Mountain Air Station in Colorado Springs during the early 1990s I did a web search on Sherlock Holmes. There were quite a few societies that were on that dot-matrix print out. One of them was Doctor Watson's Neglected Patients (DWNP)

in Denver, Colorado. At that time Denver was a long drive away and gas was expensive on an airman's pay, so I did not attend any meetings.

At this time in the Air Force, I started using one of the benefits, tuition assistance, to attend Pikes Peak Community College and work towards an associate's degree in criminal justice as I was a Security Policeman in the Air Force. During some of the classes there were references to Sherlock Holmes, but I just can't remember what exactly they were. One class that I took that I loved and that still sticks with me to this day is Fingerprinting. I still have the FBI fingerprint training manual we had to purchase for the class and I reference it every now and then.

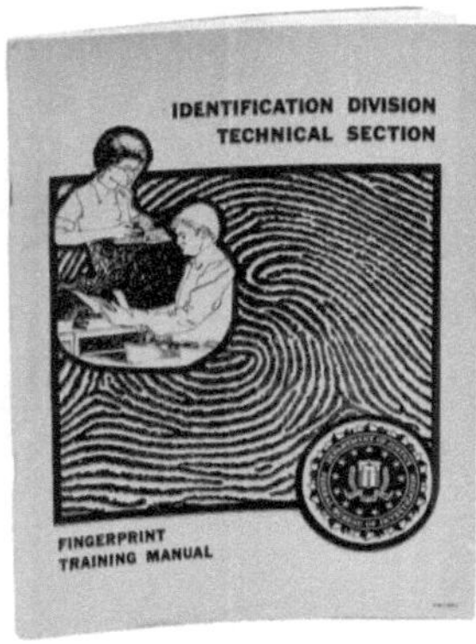

The next meeting of Sherlock Holmes that I can remember is when I was browsing the McKinzey-White bookstore in Colorado Springs and came across Issue 38 of *Sherlock Holmes, The Detective Magazine* in 2000. I am not sure why I purchased it other than it was Sherlock Holmes and it piqued my curiosity once again.

I received an honorable discharge from the Air Force in December of 1995 and decided to use my GI Bill benefits to attend the University of Colorado, Colorado Springs in the fall of 1996. I am not sure about the year, but I was in the college library looking for books I needed for some classes, and I came across a book that seemed out of place. It was called *Mystery and Detection, Thinking and Problem Solving with the Sleuths*. And of course, who was on the cover other than a cartoon character of Sherlock Holmes. I flipped through the pages and the table of contents, and Sherlock Holmes was mentioned in multiple places throughout the book. So, I purchased the book and enjoyed the many entries on various mystery authors, Sherlock Holmes, critical thinking, and problem-solving methods.

In 2004 and 2005, the next pieces of Sherlock Holmes influence into my life appeared was Leslie Klinger's *The New AnnotatedSherlockHolmes*. The first two volume set I found at Borders bookstore in Colorado Springs. The third volume I do not remember where I found it, but I knew I had to purchase it to complete the three-volume set, and, of course, to complete the partial silhouette of Sherlock Holmes in the deerstalker cap smoking his pipe on the individual spines of all three volumes.

I am sure most everyone remembers the release of *Sherlock Holmes* (2009 film) with Robert Downey, Jr. as Sherlock Holmes and Jude Law as Dr. John Watson. Even though many of us grew up watching Basil Rathbone or Jeremy Brett, which I admit I have not seen yet, (insert gasps, I know) it was a fresh look at the character with new twists to solving the crime presented throughout the movie. I love the slow-motion thought process of thinking through the situation. I wish all problems would slow down like that to be worked through in real life. The movie, however, did take that spark and fan it into a flame creating a whole new generation of Sherlockians or Holmesian, depending on which side of the pond you reside.

Then, not too long of a wait, but still four years later, the television series, *Elementary* (2013-19), started on CBS with yet another twist on the eccentricities of Sherlock Holmes in modern day New York City. I have heard a lot of people were skeptical at first, especially when they learned of this Sherlock's recovering drug addiction situation with a sober companion of Doctor Joan Watson. Now I love Lucy Liu, and I must admit I myself was skeptical on the series formula, but after watching a couple of episodes I was hooked and just thankful for yet more Sherlock Holmes.

Even though the new BBC *Sherlock* series, 2010-17 came before *Elementary*, I was unaware of its existence for quite a few years. I remember reading a magazine —I'm not sure which magazine — but I believe they were talking about season two and I was thinking to myself, "What! There's another Sherlock Holmes series out that I did not know about?" and "How do I get it?" I remember looking into the cable TV offerings and different networks but could not find it available. Then sometime later I think the series aired again. Either way I was hooked yet again with the fantastic opening music and the way the characters developed similarly to the original stories but with a modern twist in London.

I do not remember if it was before or after BBC *Sherlock*, but I had been following the second Guy Ritchie movie starring Robert Downey Jr. and Jude Law, *Sherlock Holmes: A Game of Shadows* in 2011. Not too many sequel movies are better than the first, but for me, this second movie was leaps and bounds ahead of the first as far as the plot and the many characters, references to the original stories and all-around grand adventures.

The best part of these television shows and movies came years later with my son. I had found a DVD of the classic Disney animated movie that I remember watching as a kid: *The Great Mouse Detective*. My son, like all other children, loved these animated movies and I remember taking him to the theater every time a new one came along that looked good. That did not take too long, 2011 saw the release of *Gnomeo and Juliet* which was a fun movie about garden gnomes coming to life. Too bad it took so long for the second one to come out: *Sherlock Gnomes*, in 2018, but it was well worth the wait and just another example of all the new and wonderful releases of Sherlock Holmes related media.

As I stated before, the best part of all this was watching these shows with my son, Christian. He did not have an interest when he was younger in *Elementary* and BBC *Sherlock*, or even the two Sherlock Holmes movies with Robert Downey, Jr. But then while watching movies after supper or on a weekend at home we watched both of the Robert Downey, Jr. movies and he liked them. I cannot remember exactly how but the next thing I knew we were watching the BBC *Sherlock*. He got a kick out of Benedict Cumberbatch's portrayal of Sherlock Holmes and the comedic situations between him and Martin Freeman's Doctor Watson and the situations they found themselves in.

Sometime during all of this I made up my mind: I needed to get more involved, learn more, and force myself to have a reason for finally reading Arthur Conan Doyle's famous literary character. So, in 2016 I made the decision and joined Doctor Watson's Neglected Patients (DWNP) in Denver, Colorado. What a revelation that was, I was a complete novice of Sherlock Holmes after reading stories and then partaking in a quiz at the monthly meet up at Pints Pub in Denver. I had a lot to learn, and watched and listened at each monthly gathering. One of the stories, however, made a profound impact. It was "The Musgrave Ritual." Now I am a huge fan of Indiana Jones, and this story had me hooked. It was a treasure hunt at its core but finding the history behind it, and the crown, made it impossible to put down.

I was unable to make my first or second DWNP annual dinners in 2017 or 2018 and was pretty disappointed, but I had two whole years of reading Sherlock Holmes adventures for the first time. Missing those first two annual dinners was more than made up for in January 2019. Our Chief Surgeon (President) at the time, Darlene Cypser, gave a spectacular presentation on my favorite story, "This Very Singular Business: Observations & Deductions on 'The Musgrave Ritual.'" My first annual dinner was very made memorable by the talk over the scientific points of the story.

The Musgrave Ritual

Topics of Discussion

- Of Oaks & Elms
- Angles from on High
- Seasoned Dates
- Rust & Reaction
- A Crowning Achievement?

During this time, another new series came out on HBO Japan in 2018 called *Miss Sherlock*. I was not too sure, but again if it was anything to do with Sherlock Holmes, I was in. For at least a year I

could not find it, but with some digging into the world of HBO, I finally found and watched it, loving every episode.

Around this time in 2019 my parents were down at their winter home Truth or Consequences, New Mexico. Due to my mom's failing health, they decided to sell their place in New Mexico and stay in Minnesota where we lived and I grew up. They had been traveling back and forth between Blackduck, Minnesota and Truth or Consequences, New Mexico for over 26 years. When they sold their place in the spring of 2020, we helped them pack up everything in a U-haul and headed to my home in Colorado Springs. As you might remember that was the start of COVID, and they were not sure about traveling back and staying in hotels along the way, so they spent two weeks at my place while I worked from home. Now, when it comes time to relaxing in the evening and watching TV there were some discussions. My mom loves the PBS mystery series of shows, my dad was more classic movies from the 50s, 60s, etc. My son and I are more modern. So somewhere in there I suggested *Miss Sherlock.* To my surprise everyone was for it. By the time we finished the series, even my dad enjoyed watching the show. Even though he made it sound like it was just okay, he was pretty engrossed in a couple of episodes. I remember that time very fondly as it was the last time they were at my home in Colorado, and we all enjoyed Sherlock Holmes together before they both passed away in 2022 and 2025.

Sometime after the start of 2023, having been a member of DWNP for a while, I started to think about how to introduce new people to the world of Sherlock Holmes that may have never read the stories such as myself, or maybe they might be a very informed

Sherlockian, but may not be aware that there is a group of like-minded people that like to meet each month, have lunch, participating in a quiz on a story from the Canon and discussing the stories all while having a great time.

Late in 2023 an opportunity presented itself and that was a chance to be on the board of directors for DWNP. I accepted the responsibility and at our annual dinner in 2024, was elected as the

Staff Surgeon (vice president) along with Derrick Belanger as the Chief Surgeon or President and five "Interns" or board members. In 2025 and 2026, I was re-elected as Staff Surgeon. 2024 was DWNP's fiftieth anniversary and I was able to help celebrate by coordinating the creation of a commemorative DWNP coin.

I was also honored to be the presenter at our 2025 annual dinner and after some technical difficulty with the projector, was able to present "Sherlock Holmes and Scouting." This was something I had been interested in doing ever since I found out that the founder of Scouting, Lieutenant-General Robert Stephenson Smyth Baden-Powell, otherwise known as Baden-Powell or BP in scouting circles, made many references to Sherlock Holmes in many of the first Scouting handbooks. While researching for the presentation I came across a lot of references connecting scouting and Sherlock Holmes, and even read a book by Jerry Riggs in which Sherlock Holmes sponsored a scout troop to the first scout gathering on Brownsea Island where he meets Baden-Powell and solves a mystery. What mystery was that? None other than "Sherlock Holmes, Return to the Musgrave Ritual." I could not believe it, my favorite story taken to a whole other level.

When Baden-Powell was teaching scouts methods in observation and deduction, he called these skills "Sherlocking" or "Sherlock Holmesism." The technique consists of eight words made up from the letters of his name. S.H.E.R.L.O.C.K. See, Hear, Examine, Read, Learn, Observe, Conclude and Know. As we all know, Sherlock Holmes was a master of observation. I won't quote it here, but go and look in "A Study in Scarlet" how Sherlock described everything you could know about someone by observing them. I plan to write another article soon taking up where my presentation on Sherlock Holmes and Scouting left off.

One thing I learned since I joined DWNP is that there is always something new to learn each time you read a story, participate in the quizzes, or take part in the discussions afterwards. There is so much to Sherlock Holmes that it is impossible to learn it all. But it is fun trying! I have decided to concentrate on the basics such as the characters, what type of case the story is, and how did Holmes solve it. Another thing I am working on is to create cheat sheets for myself such as the Jay Finley Christ abbreviations for each story. I have learned about chronology in Sherlock Holmes and the deep rabbit-hole into which one could disappear.

I am thinking about starting with those basics and then finding a couple topics that interest me, doing research on previous published scholarly works that may already address my area of interest. Having done that, I would like to start my own research in those areas I find most interesting and make it available to others interested in Sherlock Holmes scholarly works. This article is my first step in doing just that. Looking back and remembering all the instances where Sherlock Holmes and I intersected, what I have learned, and where I want that next adventure to lead.

The question remains, why did I take so long to read a Sherlock Holmes story even after watching the Basil Rathbone movies and all the other things I talked about? I guess I still somehow thought that if I read a story and I did not like it then the magic would be gone. So, imagine my surprise when I joined DWNP's and read the story,

"The Adventure of the Musgrave Ritual."

Now for the kicker, it has been nine years since I joined DWNP and you would think that I would have read every story by now. That is not entirely true. You see I have not been able to make it to every meeting since I joined. I have tried to read the stories in the month that we are meeting to discuss them, but I was not able to read them all. Plus, at the same time I have only been able to read two of the four novels. So that leaves two novels and a small number of stories yet to read for the first time. I know some of you may be saying, "What are you waiting for, you should have read them by now!" But think to yourself, don't you wish you could be in this same position, reading original Sherlock Holmes stories for the first time! I will read them all eventually, but for now, I smile at myself knowing that there are still unread Sherlock adventures yet to read for the first time.

The Bulldog of Scotland Yard

by

Karen Murdock

In "The Cardboard Box" Sherlock Holmes gives a somewhat backhanded compliment to Inspector Lestrade, his frequent Scotland Yard competitor and frenemy.[1]

> "That he [Lestrade] may be safely trusted to do, for although he is absolutely devoid of reason, he is as tenacious as a bulldog when he once understands what he has to do, and, indeed, it is just this tenacity which has brought him to the top at Scotland Yard." (CARD)

Not only is Lestrade as tenacious as a bulldog, but he even looks a little bit like a bulldog. In other stories Watson references "Lestrade's bulldog features" (SECO) and says the inspector is "a small wiry bulldog of a man" (HOUN). Other animal metaphors applied to Lestrade are a rat and a ferret,[2] so a bulldog does not seem so bad. Besides, bulldogs are a popular breed of dog, both for companionship and for college mascots.

It was not always so. Bulldogs were mentioned by name as early as the 15th century in England, and, as the name suggests, they were originally bred for the practice of "bull-baiting." This barbaric blood sport was popular in the Middle Ages. Bull-baiting involved sending dogs to attack and subdue a bull by biting and holding on to its nose or neck This often resulted in the death of the bull. Bulldogs were bred to have a low center of gravity, a muscular build, and a tenacious grip.

In 1835 England passed the Cruelty to Animals Act, one provision of which outlawed bull-baiting. At that point, breeders began to selectively breed bulldogs with a gentle disposition (but the same physical attributes). Over time, the bulldog breed was transformed into a loving, loyal, and gentle family pet. It remains a symbol of courage and tenacity, however, as evidenced by its frequent use as a mascot for sports teams.

Dog breeds which serve as school mascots in the United States include the husky, collie, wolfhound, golden retriever, bluetick coonhound, Labrador retriever, saluki, and Boston terrier. Topping all of these, the English bulldog is the most popular dog mascot. Wikipedia lists 46 American colleges and universities who have a bulldog for their mascot. These include the University of Georgia, Yale University, Mississippi State, Georgetown University, and Drake University.

There may have been an actual bulldog in the Canon, in addition to Lestrade, The Bulldog of Scotland Yard. In the first Sherlock Holmes story, "A Study in Scarlet," Watson tells his roommate-to-be, Sherlock Holmes, "I keep a bull pup and I object to rows because my nerves are shaken." (STUD)

This dog is never again heard from in the Canon. (Some Sherlockians have speculated that the animal might have succumbed to one of Holmes's chemical experiments.) Lestrade remains the only Canonical bulldog.

ENDNOTES

1. Lestrade appears in 13 of the original sixty Sherlock Holmes stories, far more than any other official police officer.

2. "There was one little sallow rat-faced, dark-eyed fellow who was introduced to me as Mr. Lestrade." (STUD) "Lestrade, lean and ferret-like as ever" (STUD)

The (Second) Napoleon of Crime and the Caped Crusader

by

Scott Tate

The year is 1946. London is in the grip of a crime wave, and Professor Moriarty is to blame. Scotland Yard is stymied, so naturally they turn to that great detective… Batman.

"Batman and Robin in Scotland Yard," appearing in Detective Comics No. 110, bore a cover date of April 1946, which means it was available at newsstands approximately three months earlier. The story brings the Dynamic Duo to London by special request of local authorities who are helpless against the crimes of someone using the familiar name of Professor Moriarty. Lacking a Holmes to call upon, officials at Scotland Yard do the next best thing, telegraphing across the Atlantic to Gotham City to request the assistance of Batman and Robin. In their civilian guises of Bruce Wayne and Dick Grayson, along with their loyal butler Alfred, they hasten to book passage in response.

Visually, the Moriarty we encounter within this story is passably reminiscent of Holmes' description of Moriarty in "The Final Problem" (FINA): "He is extremely tall and thin, his forehead domes out in a white curve, and his two eyes are deeply sunken in his head. He is clean-shaven, pale, and ascetic-looking, retaining something of the professor in his features. His shoulders are rounded from much study, and his face protrudes forward." His mild appearance beguiles the menacing nature of the mind within.

However, the story quickly makes it clear that this Moriarty is not the original Napoleon of Crime resurrected miraculously or diabolically, nor is he a genealogical descendant. In the world of this story, Holmes, Moriarty, *et al*, are considered fictional; "There never was any Sherlock Holmes, except in Conan Doyle's brain," the current Moriarty states at one point. But this Moriarty is no mere usurper of the name, as it and the professorial title are apparently his own. He is a coincidental namesake who draws criminal inspiration from his literary antecedent.

We're told that the modern Moriarty "changes the crimes of the fictional Moriarty just enough so it's no good studying the Holmes stories." What crimes would those be, exactly? The attribution of specific crimes to Moriarty within the Canon are notoriously vague. As we know from Holmes' description of his activities: "He does little himself. He only plans. But his agents are numerous and splendidly organized. Is there a crime to be done, a paper to be abstracted, we will say, a house to be rifled, a man to be removed – the word is passed to the Professor, the matter is organized and carried out" (FINA). With such broad concepts, what precisely has the modern Professor been doing? What details did he gain inspiration from, and what did he change about them?

A specific indication we receive of one of his crimes comes from a newspaper headline shown in the story: "Moriarty Strikes Again, Police Constable Is Wounded by Mobsters." Alas, this by itself is too broad to convey much. It's impossible to infer with certainty whether the hapless constable was a principal target in the plot or just an incidental victim during the perpetration of another crime. Does this Moriarty communicate with his gang via a code or cipher, as in *The Valley of Fear*? Perhaps, but we cannot assume so, as what we see in the Batman story offers nothing to either imply or preclude that. With only twelve pages for the story to express itself at a fast pace designed to satisfy young readers, we must reluctantly concede the glossing over of certain details such as the details of Moriarty's ongoing crime spree. We simply accept as a given that it has been problematic enough to warrant sending overseas for a superhero.

We can observe, however, that this Moriarty has failed to copy the original's methods in one significant way. The classic Moriarty's greatest asset, other than his innate intellect, was his anonymity and the care with which he preserved it. It took Holmes himself time before he suspected the existence of an individual functioning in Moriarty's capacity, and longer still before he determined a name to attach to the man. Even then Holmes lacked sufficient evidence to prove the matter in a court of law. In contrast, the Moriarty of 1946 operates in the open, his name not only known to the Yard but splashed across newspaper headlines as well. Perhaps he attempted secrecy at first and failed, or perhaps arrogance made him bold from the beginning. Either way, he foolishly lost what could have remained a potent tool in his chosen trade.

While Batman and Robin consult with the Yard, Bruce Wayne's butler Alfred reacquaints himself with his former home city as a tourist by making a pilgrimage to Baker Street. If the idea of Holmes as mere fiction feels sacrilegious to you, take solace in knowing that in contrast to almost everyone else in this story, Alfred is characterized as a true believer. "To Alfred, Sherlock Holmes was more than a fictional character," an omniscient narrative panel states, "he was a real person." Upon arriving at Baker Street, "a spot dear to his heart," Alfred is profoundly moved. "These flagstones once rang to the tread of Holmes's feet," he thinks to himself, "and from those windows gazed eagle eyes that missed nothing!" Alfred even dons a stereotypical deerstalker cap and Calabash pipe in honor of the occasion.

As many Sherlockians are aware, no historical record exists outside of the Canon for a Baker Street address numbered as 221B in the late nineteenth or early twentieth centuries. When street numbers were reassigned in the 1930s, Abbey House, home to what was then called the Abbey Road Building Society, was technically located at 229 Baker Street, but spanned enough of the block to physically occupy the space where a hypothetical 221 would stand. For many years they fielded the responsibility of receiving and responding to mail sent to Sherlock Holmes from all over the world. (Much later in 1990, use of 221B as a mailing address was formally granted to the nearby Sherlock Holmes Museum located slightly farther along Baker Street.) It is indeterminate exactly what physical building Alfred stood admiringly in front of, as no address number is stated or shown within the story, but it was definitely located within what one character refers to as "the Sherlock Holmes neighborhood." (Pardon the American spelling, as the speaker was most likely British-born and probably thought of the word as "neighbourhood," but the Yankee variant is how it was rendered in its printed form.)

To Alfred's bad luck and the narrative plot's convenience, Moriarty and his gang occupy a house across the street, "the last place the police would expect to find us." This isn't specifically said to be Camden House, which in "The Adventure of the Empty House" (EMPT) "stands opposite [Holmes' and Watson's] old quarters [and] commands an excellent view of that picturesque pile," but it quite possibly is, and is surely the functional equivalent thereof. Needless to say, for any devotee of the Canon this brings to mind Col. Sebastian Moran's vantage point from which he sniped at Holmes' window with his air-gun. Looking down through its window now, one of Moriarty's nervous henchmen spots the deerstalker-clad Alfred seeming to nose around outside: "Sherlock 'olmes, so help me – or his spirit!" Overreacting to the perceived threat, Moriarty orders two others of his followers to seize Alfred, which they promptly do.

A short while later, Batman and Robin arrive on the scene and observe footprints and scuffle marks, concluding in the grand tradition of Holmes that an abduction has taken place, and Robin correctly deduces that Alfred was the victim. They quickly follow the trail across the street and have their first direct confrontation with Moriarty and his crew. Moriarty and his men escape, but Alfred is rescued and the crimefighters gain a clue as to where and when the Professor will strike next.

We also see the heroes recover some stolen jewels from one of Moriarty's previous crimes. The Canon offers several cases involving gems, jewels, or jewelry, with even more serving as potential inspiration for Moriarty if he "changed the crime just enough" from other types of theft. So once again we are left with a tantalizingly vague suggestion that lacks enough data to hypothesize about the precise nature of Moriarty's crime and which adventure he based it on. All we can know is that he was successful in committing it.

The only planned crime we actually see Moriarty's gang carry out involves a signal rocket being fired from atop Victoria Tower at the Houses of Parliament, serving as a cue for a van to block traffic on Westminster Bridge in order to intercept a shipment of gold, which Moriarty's men lower by rope into a waiting boat. It's difficult to recall a Canonical adventure which might have inspired such a scheme, even allowing that some of the details have been changed… but let us try, in the spirit of the Great Game. What if Moriarty worked backwards – that is to say, what if word reached him that a gold shipment would be vulnerable in transit at a certain time and place, and he sought a Canonical connection to rationalize striking there? If so, possibly he recalled "The Adventure of the Second Stain," in which a crime took place "almost in the shadow of the great Tower of the Houses of Parliament." Or perhaps it was instead "The Adventure of the Bruce-Partington Plans," an occasion on which Watson recorded that he and Holmes "drove swiftly past the Houses of Parliament and over Westminster Bridge." Neither of those tales are traditionally associated with Moriarty, but perhaps the Moriarty of 1946 stretched the point out of greed. It's conceivable he is even a dabbler in the Great Game himself, hypothesizing the original Moriarty's guiding hand operating behind the scenes in some tales, as many Sherlockian scholars have suggested over the years. Or perhaps its even possible that the Canon as it is known in Batman's world reads a bit differently in some of its details than it does in our own.

Later, Batman borrows a trick from EMPT himself, even though by that point in the story the scene of the action has moved away from Moriarty's gang occupying Camden House or its equivalent. He positions a misleading bust to draw gunfire away from the intended target of his own head, much as Holmes did to lure out Moran.

There's one more connection here to FINA that probably wasn't intended as such. The name Mortimer appears several times across the Canon in various contexts: Dr. James Mortimer in HOUN, Mortimer Tregennis in WIST, Mortimer Maberley in 3GAB, a tobacconist in REDH, and a gardener in GOLD. But of particular interest to us in connection to one of the Moriarty stories is a place rather than a person: Mortimer Street, passingly mentioned in FINA ("clambering over the wall which leads into Mortimer Street"). Here in the Batman story, at one point a delivery lorry can be seen briefly in the foreground, with the name "Mortimer" clearly visible on its side. One obvious implication is that it represents a business based on Mortimer Street, which is located down Marylebone Road from Baker Street.

However, the real reason for the truck's signage is more mundane: The artist who illustrated this story also has the surname Mortimer. As per a contractual obligation at the time, credit for the story's artwork was officially attributed to Batman's creator Bob Kane, but in fact Win Mortimer performed most or all of the drawing and inking duties on this story, and possibly served as the colorist as well. Because he received no public credit for his contributions at the time, he indulged in the time-honored tradition practiced by many anonymous artists in his field, slipping his name into the artwork as a signature in the form of the business name on the truck. His given name is also hidden earlier in the story in the form of a storefront called Winslow Antiques. It's possible that Win Mortimer wasn't aware when he incorporated his name into this story that it also appeared in FINA, but it's a pleasing coincidence nonetheless.

James Winslow Mortimer (1919-1998), usually referred to as Win Mortimer, was a Canadian artist who began working for the publisher of the Batman stories, DC Comics, in 1945, only a few months prior to this story. He later also occasionally freelanced for other publishers, including Gold Key Comics and a memorable span of Spider-Man stories for Marvel between 1974 and 1982. Characters of note he co-created include the Knight and Squire, a pair of English-born heroes introduced in 1950 who openly borrow their crime-fighting style and methods from Batman and Robin as their role models. If the Knight and Squire had existed at the time of this story, Batman and Robin might not have had to travel to London.

The story's writer, Donald Clough Cameron (1905-1954), was a former crime reporter for the Detroit Free Press and later a reporter for the Winsor Star of Ontario, Canada. He also authored a handful of pulp novels, some under the nom de plume C.A.M. Donne, with delightfully lurid titles such as *Isle of Ghouls* and *Vengeance of the Severed Hands*. In his comic book career, notable characters he created include Alfred Beagle (the earliest version of Bruce Wayne's butler before he became more enduringly known as Alfred Pennyworth), a recurring Batman foe called the Cavalier, patriotic superheroine Liberty Belle, and the original incarnation of what eventually became an entire legacy of Superman villains, each known as the Toyman.

One more of Cameron's lasting contributions comes in this very story: the first appearance of what would become a recurring vehicle at Batman's disposal. In order to facilitate Batman's and Robin's travels within London while lacking their usual Batmobile, authorities arranged for him the use of "the strangest craft that ever rode the River Thames": H.M.S. Batboat, a custom-built craft painted in Batman's signature dark blue and equipped with specialized gear. In the coming years, Batman would continue to utilize this and subsequent Batboats alongside other proprietary craft such as the Batplane and Batcopter.

In the end, Moriarty is inevitably brought to justice by Batman, who modestly shuns credit for himself and declares it as a triumph for Scotland Yard. In turn, a representative of the Yard states that the "brave and brilliant spirit" of Holmes lives on through people like

Batman and Robin.

Many years later, in Detective Comics No. 572 (cover dated March 1987), Batman and some of his allies returned to London to confront yet another villainous Moriarty, this one apparently a genuine descendant from the same family line as the original, a great-grandnephew planning an assassination attempt against the royal family. At the end of that adventure, Batman was privileged to meet Sherlock Holmes himself, elderly but no less mentally agile than ever, and most certainly real. The 1987 story isn't a direct sequel to the 1946 one and makes no mention of those earlier events at all, but it might be considered a legacy in the same vein nonetheless.

But Detective 572 is a story for another time. For now, let us take satisfaction in knowing that the sentiment once expressed by Holmes in FINA holds true for Batman as well: "But I could not rest, Watson, I could not sit quiet in my chair, if I though that such a man as Professor Moriarty were walking the streets of London unchallenged."

Lament of the Tea Brokers of Mincing Lane for Dr. Watson's Neglected Teacup

by

Lauren Cercone

As an English gentleman
(I believe we can agree)
Dr. Watson definitely
Is for us the epitome.

One fixed point in a changing age –
Yet we note this unorthodoxy.
Oh why, we must ask, does not he
Prefer to drink good English tea?

When Mrs. H sends breakfast up
Or provides sustenance hastily
More likely than some fragrant tea
Comes the steaming pot of coffee.

Miss Burnet at Wisteria Lodge
Was drugged with opium but we see
He forswears brandy and ignores tea
And opts for cups of strongest coffee.

We Brokers unabashedly
Covet the cups of Mandalay Blue
From which Brett and Burke and Hardwicke too
Sipped their much-loved morning brew

Of Arabica or dark Robusta -
Not Darjeeling or Assam
Nor Earl Grey, Pu'er, nor Yunnan,
No Oolong, Sencha, or Keemun.

When the doctor was at home
Did Mary insist on serving tea?
Perhaps that is the reason he
So oft returned to 221B.

How Much Did It Cost to Live at 221B Baker Street?

by

Alexander E. Braun

When we contemplate the Duke of Holdernesse's £6,000 (or was it £12,000?) check he gave Sherlock Holmes in "The Adventure of the Priory School" from a perspective stretching well over a century, we foggily realize that it was a considerable sum, because even with today's devalued currencies, those amounts are still nothing to sniff at. This fee, one of the few explicitly mentioned in the Canon, underscores Holmes' value to the elite; the Duke, desperate to recover his son and avoid scandal, paid handsomely for results and discretion. Back then such a sum could fund a lavish lifestyle for years.

But how much was it, really? How does one approximate a reasonable worth—the true purchasing power—of an 1895 pound sterling vis-à-vis today's ephemeral, digitized Potemkin currency? A widely accepted value of a Victorian pound in today's money is $100. This always seemed grossly undervalued to me, so I investigated its soundness. At first, I naïvely thought it would be a problem of simple solution because before and during canonical times the price of gold was astonishing stable. Yet, as economists note, while gold provided a nominal anchor, real purchasing power varied due to factors like wage growth and technological advancements.

When Sir Isaac Newton became master of the English Mint in 1717 he set gold's price at £3 17s 10d per troy ounce ($20 back then)—roughly equivalent to $5,000 as of this writing. Except for the period during the Napoleonic wars, from 1798 to 1821, the gold price set by Sir Isaac remained remarkably constant until 1914. Britain's adherence to the gold standard from 1821 onward ensured that the pound's value was tied to a fixed quantity of gold, fostering international trade confidence during the height of the British Empire.

Simplicity itself! Just divide today's gold price by its value in 1895, then use the result as a multiplier to arrive at today's equivalent. Thus, $5,000 divided by $20, gives $250. This approximates the estimate generally used to align the two currencies. More sophisticated methods, such as those from the Measuring Worth project, incorporate relative income values and commodity baskets, yield equivalents closer to $150 to $200 for labor or project costs, reflecting how a pound bought more in terms of skilled work or durable goods.

However, it soon became apparent a plethora of other variables should be included in the equation. Purchasing power parity (PPP) calculations, for instance, must account for structural economic shifts, like the rise of mass-produced goods unavailable in the 1890s.

This quest to develop a more accurate exchange rate required a deep venture into the dark domains of mathematics, Kentucky windage, and black magic.

A major hurdle is that the product range produced by past economies differs from today's, complicating purchasing power parity calculations. Comparing Victorian luxuries to modern necessities is like equating a horse-drawn carriage to an Uber ride—both transport, but are worlds apart in efficiency and cost.

For example, in Julius Cæsar's time a Roman aureus contained

8 grams of gold; going by today's gold prices that would be about $1,365.00. But bullion is one thing, purchasing power another. How does one align an aureus with today's dollar while compensating for vast differences in economies, labor, goods, and customs? From what we know about those times, an aureus could buy a significant amount of grain, pay a legionary's salary for months, or purchase a high-quality tunic.

So, while today the bullion value of an aureus might be around $1,365.00, its actual purchasing power in ancient Rome was far more than that, depending on the specific goods and services being compared. The truth is that it is next to impossible to accurately gauge this, considering that aurei circulated during a time when foot soldiers were satisfied with being paid in salt (*salarium*, from which our word "salary" originates), and taxes were usually collected in beef or grain. How does one compare the price of a good slave to, say, that of an automobile? And if so, which one—a Kia or a Rolls Royce?

Something apparently as simple as the price of food differed wildly during the times of Sherlock Holmes and Doctor John H. Watson.

In a 2012 article the British newspaper, *The Mail,* attempted to compare Victorian food prices. It concluded that adjusted for inflation today's overall grocery prices are 8,553% lower today. The writer estimated that Victorian shoppers would have needed £1,254 in today's currency to fill a weekly basket with a selected range of food, drink, and household items, compared to about £120 in 2012. This disparity arose from seasonal scarcities and transportation costs; for instance, fresh produce was a luxury for urban dwellers, often preserved in costly ways like canning or pickling.

The newspaper selected 33 items such as a dozen eggs, chocolate, a loaf of bread, a toothbrush, a bottle of sherry, and applied an average earnings measure of inflation to Victorian prices. Eggs, for example, cost 1s per dozen in 1890 (about £6 in 2012), while a modern dozen might run £2 to £3, reflecting refrigeration and industrial farming's impact. The biggest differences were non-native fruits—far more costly back then. A pineapple that cost about £2 ($2.70) in 2012 sold for five shillings in 1862, estimated by the magazine to be £180. The price of 2.2 pounds (1 kg) of grapes has dropped 7,419%, while a melon's fell by 5,972%, bread 451%, butter 1,138%, tea 2713%.

The newspaper, however, did not consider that it is not only the passing of time that makes the same items considerably differ in value. For example, a respected homemaker's manual of the time warned that it was in very bad taste to feed your servants lobster more often than twice a week. Lobster, once a cheap "poor man's protein," later became a fashionable delicacy in Victorian Britain, fetching up to 3s per pound by the 1890s—£15 today.

The availability and price of the ungainly crustacean have greatly altered since then. Generally, Victorian grocery shoppers spent a third or more of their earnings on food. Compare this to today, when groceries account for about 15% of our weekly spending. A main reason for this is that wages have risen tenfold, while technological changes have made food from around the world economically available.

Towards the end of the 19th century developments such as practical refrigeration changed matters. This allowed considerably cheaper butter and mutton from New Zealand to be shipped, as well as beef from Argentina and the U.S.A. The first refrigerated ship, the SS *Strathleven*, arrived in 1879, within a decade slashing import costs by 40% and stabilizing working-class diets prices.

Another factor significantly enhancing Victorian purchasing power was an absurdly low income tax. Introduced in 1842 to great controversy by Prime Minister Robert Peel, the tax rate was set at 8d per pound, approximately 3.33%. Contrast that to the piratical 27% income tax rate paid by the average American. To top it off, only incomes above a certain threshold were taxed, which at the time was set at £160; most Victorians earned considerably less. By 1894, the threshold rose to £160 to £200, exempting 90% of the population, while higher earner rates peaked at 5d per pound for incomes over £2,000. Also, there were no general sales taxes—in the United States a gallon of gasoline is subject to five separate taxes. Instead, the government relied on other forms of taxation—often tariffs—to generate revenue, including excise duties on specific goods, such as alcohol and tobacco. Spirits, for instance, bore duties up to 20s per gallon, funding a third of the national budget by 1890.

In "The Adventure of the Second Stain," referring to the possible cost of retrieving the missing letter from the spy holding it, Holmes alludes to taxes: "The situation is desperate, but not hopeless. Even now, if we could be sure which of them has taken it, it is just possible that it has not yet passed out of his hands. After all, it is a question of money with these fellows, and I have the British Treasury behind me. If it's on the market I'll buy it—*if it means another penny on the income-tax*," [italics mine]. This quip reflects Holmes' wry awareness of fiscal policy; a "penny on the income-tax" would have doubled rates for many. When he speaks of "another penny on the income-tax," he is greatly exaggerating.

Working the Problem

To estimate the value of a pound sterling during Queen Victoria's reign and well into the Edwardian Era in today's dollars, I resorted to historical currency conversions and available inflation data. Reliable tools like the Bank of England's inflation calculator peg a 1900 £1 at £130 to £140 today, or about $190 at current rates, but are silent when it comes to spending power.

In Victorian times, the exchange rate was £1 = $5.00; using various historical inflation calculators, £1 from 1900 averages to about £170 today. There are other considerations; for instance, the aforementioned lower taxes and real estate prices—*i.e.,* actual purchasing power. Queen Victoria bought the luxurious Scottish Highlands Balmoral 50,000-acre estate for £30,000. It is currently estimated to be worth £49 million (approximately $63 million). That

alone establishes the true value of a Victorian pound sterling well beyond today's $100.

I used three data sources in my calculations. Amongst these was my bound collection of *The Strand Magazine*. This well-illustrated monthly periodical was Watson's principal publisher. Fortunately, alongside its content its pages included advertisements — with prices — for products and services appealing to its middle-class readership; bicycles for £10 to £15, tailoring at 2 guineas per suit are revealing costs.

My second and most valuable source was the *1897 Sears Roebuck & Company Catalogue*; its 708 pages provided prices for practically every everyday use item, from sundries to pianos to horse-drawn carriages, guns, corsets, jewelry, and kitchen implements. A parlor organ at $39.50 equated to £8, while a shotgun at $5.75 (£1.15) suited country pursuits like those in "The Adventure of the Gloria Scott."

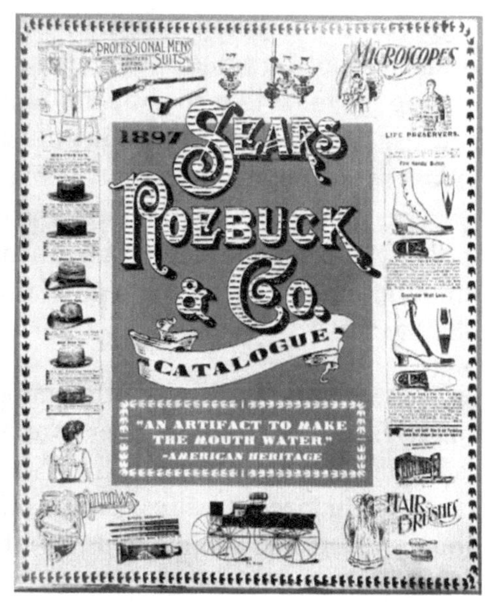

Through The Library of Congress I accessed issues of *The Times,* published during the latter half of the 19th century, offering classifieds for servants at £20 to £40 annually and horses at £30 to £50.

After months of research, using price data equivalences of over a thousand different items, including wages, I concluded that a more accurate rate of exchange between an 1890 pound sterling and today's dollar is £1 = $375.00. Other considerations contributed to this figure, including the era's lower healthcare costs —Victorian doctors often bartered services—and robust public transport, with omnibus fares at 1d per mile.

A Matter of Wages

To determine a currency's value, wages must be considered. In Victorian times, a skilled worker might earn about £1 per week, which covered rent, food, and other necessities. Clerks averaged 25s to £2 weekly, while engineers reached £3 to £4, per Board of Trade reports.

Assuming our old friend, Scotland Yard's Giles Lestrade was at the highest pay rate level for a Chief Inspector, he would have earned £2 8s per week, or £150 16s a year (≈$56,600 today). A constable was paid 32s per week, or £83 4s per year (≈$31,200). These figures, from 1890 police pay scales, placed inspectors among the upper working class, affording modest homes in suburbs like Kensal Green.

As mentioned, a major contributing factor to the currency's

high value was gold's stability. Until the early 20th century, most countries tied the value of their currency to the gold standard, directly linking its value to a specific amount of gold. This ensured stability because coins were stamped in gold and banknotes were redeemable in that same metal. Governments maintained strict control over gold reserves and monetary policies, ensuring that the gold standard was globally accepted, avoiding significant price fluctuations. This kept inflation under control, with annual rates averaging under 1% from 1870 to 1913.

Pax Britannica was another support of this economic stability. Great Britain's triumph over Napoleon Bonaparte established it as what we today would call a "superpower." Through a Gordian knot of alliances, treaties, and familial relations with other royal houses, England maintained an often uneasy peace in Europe. While Britannia ruled the waves the mighty Royal Navy was the iron fist in the silken glove that balanced European power, further stabilizing global gold-based economies, resulting in steady growth. The period's low volatility in bond yields, as seen in consol prices, reflected investor confidence in Britain's naval dominance and colonial trade networks, which handled 25% of world exports by 1900.

Gold value and demand remained stable until 1914, with the beginning of the First World War and the subsequent abandonment of a strict gold standard to enable warring countries to spend more than they had by printing gold-unsupported money. Britain's suspension in 1914 led to a 50% inflation spike by 1920, eroding the pound's post-war strength.

The Resources of Holmes and Watson

Like any great city—now or in 1895—Imperial London was expensive, particularly for someone of limited resources whose rank demanded surroundings above those of the working class. Marylebone, home to Baker Street, was a respectable but not extravagant district; comparable lodgings in 1881 rented for £80 to £120 annually, per *The Times* ads, covering two bedrooms and a sitting room with fireplaces.

Living very economically would have made it impossible to sustain Holmes and Watson's social rank. Thus, the Baker Street pied-à-terre was ideal. It was within walking distance of the great city's center, allowing convenient client access. In view of the accommodations and price levels, our friends probably split a yearly rent of £200 (≈$75,000), which included food and laundry. Mrs. Hudson's inclusive terms, as Watson notes, were a boon; typically, landladies charged extra for meals at 1s 6d daily.

Although we are uncertain about Holmes' resources at the time they could not have been very ample considering that he alone was unable to afford 221B's rent.

This lamentable situation was not long-lasting. By 1890, Holmes paid "princely" sums for his digs, leading Watson to observe, ". . . the rooms might have been purchased at the price." We know little about Holmes' fees. His haughty claim to millionaire Neil Gibson in "The Problem of Thor Bridge" that, "My professional charges are upon a fixed scale. I do not vary them, save when I remit them altogether," is somewhat equivocal; based on parallels with detectives like Pinkerton agents who charged £100+ for complex inquiries, this "fixed scale" likely ranged £50 to £500 per case for private clients.

The canonical cases are practically mute regarding the Great Detective's fees. We know that the Duke of Holdernesse gave him a check for £6,000—possibly £12,000. Well-invested either amount would have been sufficient to retire on. It is difficult to accept that his vaunted "fixed scale" was so inflexible. Other hints include £500 (implied) from the King in "A Scandal in Bohemia" and reimbursements for expenses in cases like "The Blue Carbuncle," suggesting a portfolio income exceeding £5,000 annually by the 1890s—top 1% territory.

Unfortunately, we are unaware what fees might have resulted from the 140 or so lost cases mentioned in passing by Watson. Considering that he was consulted by a Pope, royal families, nobility, and high government officials and that, as Holmes admitted nonchalantly, his practice extended beyond Britain, his earnings must have been nothing short of magnificent. International cases, like the 1891 Moriarty pursuit, very likely yielded diplomatic gratuities, bolstering his Reichenbach-era solvency. This explains how he could afford to take some cases merely because they interested him although there might be no fee involved; It's a certainty that he did not get a brass farthing from the official police.

At the Great Friendship's beginning, Watson's economical situation was no better. In *A Study in Scarlet* he reveals that "I had neither kith nor kin in England, and was therefore as free as air—or as free as an income of eleven shillings and sixpence a day will permit a man to be." He was trying to subsist on £17 5s per month, or about $84,000 per year. His Afghan wound pension, granted under the 1879 Royal Warrant, was inadequate for London.

In time, Watson's money worries faded. In "The Adventure of Shoscombe Old Place," when Holmes asked if he knew anything about the turf, he casually replied, "I ought to. I pay for it with about half my wound pension"—some $32,000 today, making what was once his only source of money mere disposable income. (However, I have always suspected that our medico exaggerated just a trifle the cost of this vice.)

Aside from the writing fees derived from The Strand— £50 per story initially, rising to £100 by *The Hound of the Baskervilles*, netting £2,000+ over the decade—as a gentleman physician Watson would have received a fee of one guinea (≈$390) per visit. A consultant (what we today call a specialist) like Trevelyan in "The Adventure of the Resident Patient" earned between 3g (≈$1,200) and 5g (≈$2,000). If we average his fee to $1,600 per patient, and posit that he daily attended to two patients, this would equal a yearly earning of some $840,000.

A successful socially prominent practice could make a man rich. Such a doctor might earn £1000 to £2000 (≈$380,000 to $750,000) a year. An ordinary general practitioner, however, had an income similar to that of other middle-class workers, 5s (≈$95) per visit, although most doctors charged only 2s 6d (≈$50). Upper-tier surgeons like Watson, with military credentials, commanded guineas from Mayfair patients.

Watson inhabited his profession's upper societal regions. As a surgeon he merited the title of "doctor"—important for several reasons. Doctors were considered gentlemen; their wives could be presented at court. Other physicians or apothecaries' ladies would not, because those men had been trained through apprenticeship and therefore engaged in what was considered manual labor. Consider this exchange between Holmes and James Mortimer in *The Hound of the Baskervilles*: "And now, Dr. James Mortimer—" "Mister, sir, Mister—a humble M.R.C.S." This snobbery stemmed from the 1858 Medical Act, which professionalized medicine but preserved hierarchies; M.D. holders from places like the University of London (Watson's alma mater) dined in the front parlor; apothecaries used the tradesmen's entrance.

This effort, with its satisfying results, opened for me yet another window (albeit a small one) into 1895, affording a further glimpse into the lives of our two friends. Considerable personal satisfaction may be derived from this minor accomplishment—for instance, it is pleasing to know that the sovereign Irene Adler gave Holmes for serving as a much-needed witness to her wedding, which he forever carried linked to his watch chain, although not treasured for its intrinsic value, is worth $375 today.

Seneca put it best: *Scientia inutilis utilium rerum ignorantia melior est.* (The knowledge of useless things is better than the ignorance of useful things.)

The "TANKS."
By Col. E. D. SWINTON.
FIRST AUTHORITATIVE ACCOUNT.
Drink
FRY'S
COCOA
See Page 27.
SOUTHAMPTON STREET
THE STRAND MAGAZINE
SHERLOCK HOLMES
Outwits
A GERMAN SPY
You can send this Magazine Post Free to the Troops.
See Page 320.
Nº 321
VOL 54
8d. net.
SEPTEMBER, 1917.

A Short Quiz for Geniuses on "The Five Orange Pips"

by

Larry Feldman

Part I - The Unrecorded Cases Mentioned in "The Five Orange Pips"

Instructions: Match the Unrecorded Cases mentioned in FIVE listed below to the blank space in the following list.

a) Lost British Bark

b) Amateur Mendicant

c) Camberwell

d) Chamber

e) Tankerville

f) Uffa

1)________What was the item named after Paradol?

2)________What society held a luxurious club in a furniture warehouse?

3)________Where might we find the Grice-Patersons?

4)________Where did the infamous poisoning case take place?

5)________Who was Sophy Anderson and what happened to her?

6)________What club scandal involved Major Prendergast?

Part II – The Case

1) There are two things the client wants from Holmes. According to Holmes, the first is "easily got" and the second is "not so easy". Name them.

2) What two inventions contributed to the success of Joseph Openshaw's factory in Coventry?

3) Was the Lone Star a steam ship or a sailing ship? How does Holmes deduce the answer?

4) Name two things that Holmes "tore to pieces" and where he found each of them.

5) List the five verbs used to describe the wind at the outset of the story?

The answer keys to both quizzes are on p. 46

"HIS EYES BENT UPON THE GLOW OF THE FIRE."

Answer Keys to Quizzes on "The Five Orange Pips."

Key to Part I

1) d

2) b

3) f

4) c

5) a

6) e

Key to Part II

1) Advice and Help

2) The bicycle and the Openshaw Unbreakable Tire

3) The time differences between the arrival of the letters and the murders.

4) Loaf of bread from the sideboard, an orange from the cupboard.

5) Screamed, shrieked, cried, sobbed, and howled.

The Protestant Dilemma

by

Todd R. Sciore

As I had some clandestine business this morning at the newsstand a few streets over, I rose earlier than normal and was able to exit our flat at 221B Baker Street before Holmes could inquire as to my destination, or worse yet, dictate it altogether. It was a bright day, at least by London standards, where if it wasn't raining, it was about to, and the open air did my lungs a world of good after being subjected to a pungent new blend of Holmes' pipe tobacco the previous evening. The short jaunt was rather quick and unremarkable except for a collision on my return trip with an old drunkard who, after nearly knocking me to the ground, had the audacity to ask for a crown. I proceeded to admonish the man on his poor manners as he stumbled off in pursuit of his next drink, or victim, or both. With that unpleasant bit of business over, I picked up my hat, straightened my coat and continued back to our lodgings.

I quietly entered our rooms to find Holmes seated at the breakfast table deeply engrossed in the morning paper. I grabbed my medical journal and set it on our dining table, while offering my usual morning greeting and delving into the hearty breakfast that our landlady Mrs. Hudson expertly prepared. As his attention was fixed on the newspaper, I thought I might attempt a conversation by commenting on his choice of reading material.

"A bit out of character for you, Holmes, reading an American fish wrapper."

"All the news that's fit to print my dear Watson, as well as much that isn't," Holmes replied sharply, barely looking over the top of the paper to acknowledge my presence of not more than an arm's length away.

"Nothing of interest in the *Telegraph*?" I asked rather benignly, which would soon become a regrettable line of questioning.

"With London's criminal element completely lacking in both ambition and imagination lately, I have had to rely on news of illicit activities from across the pond to stimulate the senses, unlike you who chooses to keep his mind sharp by studying thoroughbred racing forms."

Now the paper was lowered slightly and as his gaze grew more piercing, I could see a sardonic smile start to cross his tightly drawn, hawk-like face.

"By Jove!" I exclaimed, having been put on the defensive, "You know I gave up my penchant for games of chance some years back and to think the contrary is purely an outrage."

"What I do know, my dear Watson, is that a thrill seeker never truly stops seeking thrills and that your ability to bluff, as they say, is as unconvincing now as it ever was."

"I dare say, Holmes, that after all of these years you still think I am frittering away my pension, a well-deserved one, mind you, on thoroughbreds? I cannot, for the life of me, see how you could come to such a preposterous conclusion."

"Then allow me to demonstrate," he said, slowly folding and setting aside the newspaper.

Holmes now gave me his full attention which, mind you, I didn't want, as I was feeling a sudden sense of guilt mixed with the lingering pangs of hunger from having not eaten since our meager dinner the previous evening.

"The ink stain on your fingers is from the recent handling of fresh newsprint yet you asked if there was anything of interest in the *Telegraph.*"

"That's hardly a conviction," I quickly replied with a false sense that I may be able to outwit him and peaceably go about my breakfasting. "I could have held any number of daily papers other than the *Telegraph* and merely inquired as to its contents as I am unaware of them."

"You then entered the flat and made straight for your medical journal which, despite your frequent reading from April to October of each year, has a page marker that has failed to move in well over three years' time. You appear to diligently make notes in the margins, yet I am sure that if I were to open it to the marked page, I would find no writing of any kind. It also features the binding work of an early edition that has no doubt been rendered obsolete by advancements in the science of medicine. Now, would you care to remove the newly purchased racing form from the book or shall I?"

Red-faced and defeated, I opened the book and pulled out my race handicapping form mumbling to myself about the difficulties of living with such a man as Holmes when he added a final insult to injury delivered with a fiendish smile.

"And as final support to my—as you call it—preposterous conclusion, the well-placed mirror and polished lamp fixture in the sitting room allows the occupant of my usual seat to not only see if the occupants of other seats are concealing a weapon behind a sheaf of papers, but also allows me to see what someone is, or as in your case, is not reading."

"Holmes, I must say you are truly a most remarkable fellow, one of a kind!" I declared, shaking my head in astonishment and all I could do was laugh out loud, while mentally making a note to check what other unknown advantages Holmes' favorite seat offers him.

I proceeded to eat my breakfast while Holmes unfolded and then began to read today's edition of the *Telegraph* lamenting that it only contained stories of "bit fakers, bludgers and bug hunters" whose crimes were "hardly worth the cost of paper and ink."

At that instant Mrs. Hudson entered our rooms to advise that there was a male visitor in the foyer who wished to speak with Mr. Holmes. While unexpected visitors to our rooms were not an uncommon event, one at such an early hour did arouse some curiosity on the part of both Holmes and myself. Intrigued, Holmes told our landlady to "show him up" and headed to occupy his favorite perch before our unknown guest arrived.

Like the Jezail bullet that wounded me all those years ago, it hit me quickly and I turned to Holmes asking, "How did you get a copy of today's *Telegraph*?"

"If you are accusing me of petty theft Watson, I'll have you know I purchased it this morning with my own funds," he replied in a sarcastic tone.

"But I rose before you and did not see you while I was out and about."

"Certainly you did, my dear Watson, and your coin purse is back on your night stand," he replied with a Cheshire cat like grin, pointing a long, bony finger in the direction of my room. I patted my empty pocket in shock, but before I could reply, Mrs. Hudson arrived with our caller who was a well-dressed, middle-aged man who introduced himself as a Mr. Shropsford of Abingdon.

"Good morning and do come in," said Holmes waving him to a chair asking, "How may I and my esteemed colleague, Doctor Watson, be of service to you?"

"Mr. Holmes, I appreciate your willingness to see me unannounced and at such an early hour," the man began. "My wife suggested that I come directly to you with a matter regarding the recent and peculiar behavior of our solicitor of several years, Mr. Jonathan Redfern," the man continued in a somewhat nervous fashion.

"In my experience, the words solicitor and peculiar are often interchangeable," Holmes replied in a smiling manner which gave our guest a slight chuckle and helped to put him somewhat at ease.

"You see, Mr. Holmes, I am a man of means," he continued.

"The cut of your suit is the style of Beacon and Landis, outfitter to London's upper class and is expertly done," said Holmes adding, "Your hands show no evidence of having performed manual labor and you have no visible hallmarks of being actively engaged in a profession so I will guess that the source of your wealth is inherited and most likely from your wife's relations," as if the man's life story were printed across his brow.

"I am not ashamed to admit you are correct. My wife was left a healthy share of her grandfather's highly successful mercantile and shipping business," Mr. Shropsford replied, a bit awestruck, as most who find themselves in my friend's company for the first time usually are.

"Rest assured I meant no shame in my observations, please carry on. Surely there is more to your seeking me out because your solicitor seems a bit off."

"There is. You see, my wife and I are large benefactors to Saint Helen's church and we recently approached Mr. Redfern about revising our testamentary papers. We simply wished to redirect a small portion of our future church bequests to a few of our secular causes and he began a thunderous tirade on the protestant dilemma, and refused to make the changes," the man replied.

"The protestant dilemma?" I asked, looking at Holmes inquisitively.

"The protestant dilemma, Watson, is that basic teachings from the pulpit stress hard work and thrift. Over time, these activities will generally allow the follower to build excess capital and with it, they become desirous of objects and activities beyond the teachings that provided them with their favorable station in life. In short, if one strictly adheres to the teachings of the church, it will enable them to stray from the church's teachings."

"Quite a conundrum," I replied.

“Indeed,” said Holmes looking at Mr. Shropsford, “and while I find it odd that it matters to your solicitor how you divide up your estate, I do not see how I can be of any assistance beyond suggesting you find someone else to handle your legal affairs.”

“Sound advice indeed but Mr. Redfern came highly recommended by Reverend Rawley at Saint Helens. Here is the peculiar part, Mr. Holmes,” our guest continued, “My wife seems to think there is a connection between Mr. Redfern and Reverend Rawley. So much so that she believes them to be one and the same person.”

Holmes sat back in his armchair for a moment with a pensive look on his face while gently packing the bowl of his pipe.

“I shall say, that is an interesting theory,” he added while striking a match and charring the tobacco.

After another moment of silence puffing on his pipe, Holmes leaned forward and said, “Tell your good wife that Sherlock Holmes will look into the matter for her,” and he jumped up to shake our guest’s hand and see him out of our flat. A spark of energy had returned to Holmes’ eyes as he contemplated Mrs. Shropsford’s theory all afternoon and mentally laid out his investigation plan.

The next day after an early breakfast, Holmes and I set off for Abingdon by cab and made our way into town around midday to call on Mr. Redfern's office. Disguised in a well-tailored suit, gold pocket watch and hand-carved walking stick, Holmes presented himself as a wealthy gentleman in need of help putting his estate in order. As we approached our destination, we disembarked from the cab. Holmes went inside while my role was to merely observe the building from a distance. After a short while I saw Holmes emerge and we took up a position that would afford us an unobstructed view while not being seen by anyone exiting the solicitor's office.

Holmes described Mr. Redfern as "A portly fellow of average height who appeared unfamiliar with manual labor yet, despite his soft and peculiar appearance, he had a deep, masculine voice that belied his bookish features."

"I could tell he is a practiced orator," noted Holmes as he described their interaction in detail.

"May I help you, Sir?" inquired the solicitor as Holmes had entered the building.

"We shall see," said Holmes in a tone befitting his disguise. "My name is Edmond Hall and I am in need of someone to assist me with getting my large and rather complicated estate in order. You came favorably recommended by someone whose opinion I value more than that of most others."

"That is very kind to hear, may I inquire who suggested you seek me out?" asked the solicitor.

"As discretion is very important to both myself and my business associates, I can only offer that he is a prominent member of Saint Helens church but nothing more," said Holmes while looking for even the slightest reaction but noticing none.

"I see. Are you also a congregant?" inquired Redfern giving Holmes a slight indication that he may have already known the answer.

"Unlike my more pious friend, I am not openly religious in my beliefs nor do I regularly pay a visit to any particular house of worship. I am more of an agnostic one might say. However, I have found my friend's counsel to be wise and he mine, thus our long friendship."

Upon hearing that, Redfern advised rather stiffly, "Unfortunately, Mr. Hall, being a practice of one man, and a rather mature one at that, I am unable to accept any new clients at this time. Perhaps a larger practice would be better suited to assist with your matters, but I truly do thank you for calling on me. Now, if you don't mind, I must be off to meet with a client who recently became a widow."

Holmes said the men then shook hands and Redfern politely showed him the door.

After a few moments, the solicitor then left the building carrying a leather attaché case.

"Watson, you discreetly follow Redfern from a distance while I go back and take a look around his office."

Knowing Holmes' skill with a set of lock picks, there was no need to inquire how he would accomplish his task while I went about mine.

I trailed Redfern to the gates of Saint Helens where he looked around before quickly entering the parsonage. I then backtracked and met up with Holmes and told him of what I saw.

"Most interesting Watson, extraordinary work. I did a little sleuthing myself. Having a good look around the office, I found his legal writing appears competent enough for the task at hand. However, I was unable to determine where Redfern attended university or conducted his legal clerkship. Inside of a locked cabinet I did find an apparent client list which I have committed to memory for further research."

"So, there is a bit of chicanery going on," I stated.

"Possibly Watson, but let us not theorize without gathering the proper data. We will know for sure soon enough. Tomorrow we will call upon Reverend Rawley at Saint Helens."

With our business done for the day, we hired a cab back to Baker Street, and, much to my delight, had a nice meal of roasted goose and vegetables courtesy of Mrs. Hudson. After dinner, Holmes sent off short notes to both his brother Mycroft and Mr. Shropsford, then we retired for the evening.

The next morning, we rose to find Mycroft's and Mr. Shropsford's written replies which Holmes read intently. After a quick breakfast, we once again headed to Abingdon. Only this time both Holmes and I were disguised as visiting clergymen. On the ride over, I voiced my thoughts on the lack of merit in misrepresenting ourselves to a real clergyman, but Holmes insisted it was necessary to our investigation. While it was hard to deny his logic, I silently hoped my attempted protests would count for something with Saint Peter when the time came. We arrived in Abingdon and first made our way past the solicitor's office Holmes had been to the day before and saw it was closed. We then made our way over to Saint Helens with Holmes providing false names to the housekeeper and requesting a brief audience with Reverend Rawley. We were shown inside the parsonage to a richly paneled waiting room where we were seated until the good Reverend entered the room. He was middle aged and a bit stocky, but thinner than the solicitor. He made our acquaintance with a deep, expressive voice with his gaze lingering on Holmes just long enough to be noticed by the trained eye. We walked the church grounds for half an hour or so discussing its history then returned inside where Holmes posed a few business minded questions about the finances required to maintain such a large property and more specifically obtaining bequests from well-heeled members.

Rawley displayed some agitation at this topic of conversation and prematurely ended our visit coolly stating, "I really must get back to preparing for this week's sermon and tending to my flock."

"Especially those sheep who may have recently lost a husband? Julia Buttonwood, I believe," replied Holmes.

Reverend Rawley's eyes widened in a flash, but he said nothing.

"Before we head back to our small, country parish, Reverend, may I kindly use your water closet?" Holmes asked innocently enough, but I knew my friend well enough to know there was a reason for asking.

"Very well, it is up the hall. When you are finished, please show yourselves out," said Rawley as he departed to his private chambers.

When Holmes emerged from the water closet, we promptly exited the church grounds and upon reaching a safe distance, he advised, "Well, Watson, the good Reverend and the solicitor are in fact one and the same".

"Are you certain, Holmes?" I asked rather incredulously.

"Not a doubt in my mind, Watson, the Solicitor's outfit was hanging in a hall closet near the water closet as I suspected it might be."

"How did you know?" I asked still trying to process a reason for the clergyman's elaborate subterfuge.

"When I met with Redfern yesterday, I noticed that his jacket had a small spot of flesh colored make up on the sleeve. I recognized the smell of it as a popular brand often used by stage actors, as well myself for certain disguises. There was a make-up kit like mine as well as a wig and a prosthetic device to make the wearer appear heavier than their true weight."

"But why the outrageous deception?"

"What better way to control the future affairs of Saint Helens than to counsel members on making bequests?" replied Holmes matter-of-factly. "Now, let us call upon the Shropsfords, but first, I am in the mood for a good meal," which got no argument from me as I was feeling a bit famished myself after the day's activities.

After enjoying a hearty platter at a nearby restaurant, we took a cab to the Shropsford home which was a grand estate of gray brick with a well-manicured, emerald green lawn, a gate house, a large circular walk and a splendid garden with various allegorical statuary visible throughout.

Introducing himself as "Mr. Sherlock Holmes of London," he asked the doorman to see if the master of the house was home, and after hearing who was at the door, we were promptly shown inside. Mr. Shropsford came down the hall, instructed the butler to bring us tea, and brought us to an elaborately decorated sitting room where we met the rather striking Mrs. Shropsford. It was she who spoke first.

"It is a pleasure to make the acquaintance of the famous Sherlock Holmes and Doctor Watson. Your reputation precedes you as the best there is at solving the unsolvable," she said in a flattering tone.

To which Holmes, surprisingly a bit taken by her elegance, replied "I assure you, the pleasure is all ours," while offering her a rare smile.

The butler entered the room with tea and biscuits arranged on a silver serving tray, placed it on the table before us and quietly exited the room, closing the ornate wooden doors and leaving only the four of us to speak in private.

"Please be seated, the both of you," Mrs. Shropsford said waving her hand towards two expensive looking chairs for us to sit on.

"Did you receive my written reply to your questions regarding familial surnames and recent member deaths at Saint Helens?" asked Mr. Shropsford.

"I did and your prompt response proved most useful, as I expected it would," replied Holmes.

"Then I trust you have some news for us regarding the story my husband told you about our solicitor and his rather untoward behavior recently?" asked Mrs. Shropsford.

Now it was Holmes' turn to lay on the flattery.

"We do, and I must admit that while most theories are just that, yours was indeed correct as to the two men being one and the same. If Scotland Yard had such intuition, crime would be eradicated," he generously added, to which the lady blushed while soaking up the compliment.

"What would make someone, especially a man of the cloth, do such a nefarious thing?" asked Mr. Shropsford.

"For the same reason many men, as well as members of the fairer sex, behave in ways far outside of their normal character when it comes to money," Holmes continued.

"Was he stealing from Saint Helens?" asked Mrs. Shropsford.

"He was not playing the crooked cross as they say. In fact, it was quite the opposite as he was merely looking out for the church's future, only in a way that was deceptive."

"Are you going to notify the authorities, Mister Holmes?"

"I feel there is no need for me to do so. It is not a crime. While a conveniently placed government official informed me that the Reverend did not possess the proper credentials to practice law, his charade was limited to members of Saint Helens and not widespread through the public at large. You may choose to call his activities to the notice of the Law Society; however, the Reverend will have a much higher authority than that to answer to for his indiscretions."

Coming somewhat to the Reverend's defense I added, "He had good intentions."

"Ahm yes, Watson, good intentions—the road to Hades is paved with them!" said Holmes, and with that we stood, said our goodbyes and left the Shropsford estate making our way back to Baker Street. The whole way home, Holmes was in a jovial mood which I dare say was more from meeting the lovely Mrs. Shropsford than from the actual solving of the case itself.

Family Law in the Canon

by

Linda Crohn and Jonathan Shimberg

As Sherlock Holmes said in "The Adventure of the Copper Beeches": "Do you know, Watson . . .that it is one of the curses of a mind with a turn like mine that I must look at everything with reference to my own special subject." While reading the Canon is entertaining and enjoying, there is no question that one of the filters we can examine the stories is through the lens of family law as many of the stories deal with family law issues. There are cases that deal with valid marriages and others with alienation of affection. Many cases showed a breach of promise to marry as well as bigamy and fraud. The laws in the later 1800's in Victorian England were not that different from the laws in America.

The first area to examine is valid marriages.

In "The Adventure of the Solitary Cyclist," the question of a valid marriage was raised. Sherlock Holmes found out that Mr. Woodley had abducted Violet Smith. Woodley had Williamson perform the marriage ceremony. When Holmes confronted them, he declared the marriage to be invalid citing three reasons. The first reason was that Williamson did not have the right to solemnize the marriage. Williamson told him that he had been ordained to which Holmes replied, "and also unfrocked." Williamson retorted "once a clergyman, always a clergyman."

Actually, Williamson is correct and Holmes is in error. According to Baring-Gould, Williamson "was accountable for such an act and open to ecclesiastical and civil action for solemnizing any marriage after his deposition." Baring-Gould goes on to quote Rev. Otis Rice, saying "the sacraments and sacramentals administered by a priest are valid whether he is inhibited, deposed, or not....Williamson might have faced disciplinary action from the church or the state for conducting the ceremony after being deposed, but nonetheless the marriage itself would have stood up under scrutiny."[1]

The next issue was whether they had a license to marry. Under the Marriage Act of 1823,[2] parties could marry by obtaining a license. The Act made substantial changes to Lord Hardwicke's Act, also known as the Clandestine Marriages Act of 1753. The 1823 Act refined and clarified the legal requirements for marriage, ensuring both parties, especially women had a say in the decision to marry. The Act also provided that a marriage would only be void if the parties "knowingly and willfully" failed to comply with certain provisions. The purpose of this provision was to invalidate only marriages that involved a deliberate flouting of the rules.

The license cost several pounds, provided for a waiting period of 15 days and required a woman's consent. A fiancé had to live in his or her parish for four weeks before the wedding, unless the Archbishop of Canterbury eliminated the waiting period by granting an immediate license. Williamson stated he had the license in his pocket. But Holmes replied that he got it by trickery. Based upon the timeline in the story, they would not have been able to comply with the waiting period requirements.

Finally, there was no consent to the marriage by Violet Smith. The law provided that a clergyman had to be notified of the couple's intention to marry a week before the banns were published.[3] Banns (or bans) were a public announcement in a Christian parish church, or in the town council, of an impending marriage between two specified persons. The banns had to be read on three successive Sundays in the parish where one of the couple resided. The purpose of reading the banns was to make the couple's intention to marry public and allow anyone to come forward who knew a reason why the couple could not lawfully marry. It is clear that the couple did not do this. And it is clear that Violet Smith did not have the intention or consent to this marriage. And if we need further proof, we need only look at the fact that she was gagged with a handkerchief.

Lest she be forgotten, Lucy Ferrier was forced to marry Enoch

Drebber in *A Study in Scarlet*. However, this article deals with English Law and not American Law.

More on valid marriages.

In "A Scandal in Bohemia," Holmes followed Irene and Godfrey to the Church of St Monica. While inside Godfrey ran toward him and said "Come, man, come, only three minutes, or it won't be legal." There has been much discussion as to why this would not be legal after the three minutes passed. The answer is under The Marriage Act of 1823[4], the ceremony needed to be performed between 8:00 a.m. and 12 noon.

Breach of Promise to Marry was an issue that was blatant in three of the cases in the canon, one that is easily argued and one that needs more explanation. The law during this period of time was as follows:

Breach of promise actions developed as an English Common Law cause of action peculiar in nature as it was a hybrid of contract law and tort law. To establish a case a plaintiff must prove 1) a promise of marriage binding on both parties, 2) the failure of the defendant to comply with that promise, and 3) damages as a result of that breach. It is important to note that the court could not compel the performance of the contract, that is, force the parties to marry (this was a change from prior English ecclesiastical law which dealt with betrothal law where a party could be ordered to marry.) Because of the personal nature of courtship and marriage, courts were more accepting of hearsay and circumstantial evidence. Without accepting such evidence this cause of action would be difficult to prove. Thus, evidence of a promise to marry could be inferred from visiting, going out together, stating an intention to a third party and the expectations of friends and family.[5]

In "The Adventure of Charles Augustus Milverton," Holmes comes charging in the room and says to Watson, "I'm engaged" to Milverton's housemaid. "I wanted information and it became a necessary step." Watson replies "But the girl, Holmes." Holmes merely shrugged his shoulders. We never hear any more of the engagement.

So, the question is: Could the housemaid prove her case? Holmes admits that he is engaged, which leads to the conclusion that she too agreed, proving the first element. We know that Holmes never intended to comply with that promise, thereby proving the second element. The problem comes to what her damages were. According to Klinger, she will be well taken care of by a rival in the household.[6] So if she marries another, she would not have any damages against Holmes. In the same footnote, Brad Keefauver is relied upon in "Sherlock and the Ladies" where he mused that Holmes could have obtained the information from her merely by romancing her. He didn't have to propose to her. He posited that perhaps the housemaid forced the proposal.

It was also clear in "A Case of Identity" that Hosmer Angel proposed to Mary Sutherland. He wanted to get married before her father came back from a business trip. She promised that she would always be true to him. The wedding was to take place in St. Savior's church near King's Cross. While she and her mother took the hansom, he got into a four-wheeler. She got to the church first and waited for him. He never came.

Again, the first two elements of breach of promise to marry were satisfied, as to Hosmer Angel, but not as to James Windibank. But what was her damage? We know that as her stepfather he couldn't and never intended to marry her. He was merely interested in having access to her money. A good lawyer could convince a jury that her broken heart, her loss of money that she gave to her parents were worth something. However, since she didn't know she had been on the receiving end of the breach of promise, there would be no recovery.

And there was never a valid enforceable contract to marry. So she couldn't recover because her stepfather was already married.

In "The Adventure of the Musgrave Ritual," we learned early on that Brunton had become engaged to Rachel Howells. He threw her over and had taken up with Janet Tregellis. Elements 1 and 2 are satisfied. This time Rachel would have had a claim for her broken heart as well as her medical expenses. But as Brunton was dead, she would not have been able to collect. What if he left an estate from which she could collect?

In "The Adventure of the Illustrious Client," Violet de Merville is engaged to Baron Adelbert Gruner. After Kitty Winter throws oil of vitriol at the Baron and the book he kept was given to Violet, "the effect at any rate, was all that could be desired." She did not marry the Baron. Could the Baron have sued her for breach of promise to marry?

The actual story of "The Adventure of the Three Gables" does not reveal any breach of promise to marry. However, while watching the Granada Television production of this story, Holmes threatens Isadora Klein with charges of the murder of Maberley. Holmes required her to break the engagement to the Duke of Lomond by Thursday. Since she was a wealthy woman, would the Duke be willing to sue her?

Bigamy was a felony under the Offences against the Person Act 1861.[7] The definition was relatively simple:

> Whosoever, being married, shall marry any other person during the life of the former husband or wife . . . shall be guilty of felony. . .

The law went on to state that it did not apply to a person whose spouse is "continually remaining beyond the seas for a space of seven years" or is absent from the other for a space of seven years, one not knowing the other to be living.

At one time such an offense was classified as a felony, and as such punishable by penal servitude for up to 7 years. Prior to this Act, the punishment was hanging. Because of the harshness of that penalty the judicial system had created the legal fiction of a defense of "benefit of clergy." If one could cite a passage in the Bible, they could claim to be a member of the clergy. As a result of that defense, the punishment was reduced to a branding on the left thumb.[8] These were replaced by the sentence of transportation to the colonies and then later to Australia and finally replace by incarceration for up to seven years.

The first case in which the issue of bigamy is encountered is "The Boscombe Valley Mystery." James McCarthy was in the clutches of a barmaid in Bristol and married her. His father was constantly goading him to marry Alice Turner, but he refused and wouldn't tell anyone why. When the barmaid read in the newspaper that he "was in serious trouble and likely to be hanged," she threw him over. She wrote to him to say that she was already married to a man in the Bermuda Dockyard. Therefore, there was no matrimonial tie between them. So, while he had refused to commit bigamy, the barmaid clearly had done so.

The story that is most connected with bigamy is "The Adventure of the Noble Bachelor." Hatty Doran married Francis (Frank) Hay Moulton. He went to seek his fortune and was believed to be captured by Apache Indians and subsequently died. Believing he was dead, Hatty agreed to marry Lord Robert St. Simon. On the way to the altar, she saw Frank and recognized him. There has been much discussion as to whether she should have stopped the wedding at that point. She decided that she didn't want to make a scene, so she went through with the marriage. The legal opinion suggested she should not have remarried.

The last case in which bigamy is raised is "The Adventure of the Yellow Face." Holmes was advised that Effie Hebron Munro had been married to an American. Holmes was told that the husband had died. But Holmes theorized that her husband was a leper or an imbecile and she fled from him. He believed that she committed bigamy when she married Grant Munro. Holmes was clearly wrong in his theory and told Watson that "if it should ever strike you that I am getting a little over-confident in my powers or giving less pains to a case than it deserves, kindly whisper 'Norbury' in my ear, and I shall be infinitely obliged to you."

In "The Adventure of the Devil's Foot," Sterndale tells Holmes for years he loved Brenda Tregennis and for years she loved him. He could not marry her, for he had a wife who has left him for years and whom, by the deplorable laws of England, he could not divorce.

The Matrimonial Causes Act[9] established only one court in London that could grant divorces and continued to make divorce unavailable to many people throughout England. Parliament was also unwilling to grant equality to the sexes on the grounds for divorce. A man could divorce his wife for one instance of adultery, but a woman could only obtain a divorce if her husband was physically cruel, incestuous, or bestial in addition to being adulterous. Since there was no adultery on either party's part, Sterndale couldn't get a divorce and therefore he could not marry Brenda Tregennis.

In *The Hound of the Baskervilles*, Laura Lyons is shocked to hear that Stapleton is married. She claimed that he offered her marriage on the condition that she could get a divorce from her husband. She had learned that there might be a way of her gaining her freedom if certain expenses could be met. She was trying to get help from Sir Charles in order to get the divorce. However, there was no indication of adultery, physical cruelty, incest or bestiality. The story only states that her life had been one of incessant persecution from her husband.

On the other hand, was Stapleton guilty of Breach of Promise to Marry? No, because he was already married.

English Common Law has long recognized remedies for a man whose wife has been lost to the arms of another.[10] An action against the person who stole his wife's affection could be brought. The wrongful taking of a spouse was considered a loss of consortium.

Consortium was defined as a bundle of rights arising out of a marital relationship, including the right to aid, comfort, society, services and exclusive sexual relations. As far back as 1692 this concept was recognized and was the basis of an award of damages. The wrong could be caused by either an intentional or negligent act. Actions for loss of consortium are alive and well in the American legal system in negligence actions even today.

At one time under Common Law, lawsuits seeking damages for criminal conversation –Adultery- against an interloper were available. However, due to abuse by plaintiffs, England as well as many states have barred those claims.

In "The Adventure of the Dancing Men," Abe Slaney clearly tried to lure Elsie Cubitt away from her husband. His attempts included threats and showing up at her home, getting mad at the offer had of money and trying to pull her through a window. Elsie was steadfast in her refusal to return to him. But if Hilton Cubitt lived would he have had an action against Slaney for trying to entice Elsie away from him?

"The Adventure of the Cardboard Box" shows Sarah Cushing trying to lure James Browner away from her sister, Mary. She went to live with James and Mary where she tried to be alone with him or coax him out for a walk. Browner accused her of poisoning his wife against him. But in England, the law applied to husband's being able to sue a man for alienating the wife's affection. It did not apply to a wife being able to sue someone for the alienation of affection of the husband.

Finally, in "The Problem of Thor Bridge," the wife, Maria Pinto thought Grace Dunbar was trying to steal the affection of her husband, Neil Gibson. She was bitterly jealous and hated Grace for the loss of her marital relationship. However, Grace was not interested in taking Gibson away from Maria. Maria would not have had a cause of action against her if she had tried, for the same reason as in "The Adventure of the Cardboard Box."

People filter their reading of the Canon with their own life experiences. Doctors may read through their filter and training based on Dr. Watson's actions. Certainly, law enforcement officers will examine the procedural aspects of Holmes and the detectives. Therapists will analyze the character's personality traits. And family law lawyers will read the stories with the filter of their training.

Family law issues were an ongoing theme in the stories. Sherlock could be named a defendant in a breach of promise action. How interesting would that be? There have been searches of English cases, but no one has been able to find the case where Agatha filed a suit against Sherlock. But the search goes on.

---

1. William Baring-Gould, *The Annotated Sherlock Holmes*, p.395 fn 12
2. 4 Geo. 4. c.76
3. Ibid.
4. Ibid.
5. Amy D'Orazio, *Breach of Promise to Marry*, May 9, 2023 found at https://www.quillsandquartos.com/post/breach-of-promise-to-marry
6. *The New Annotated Sherlock Holmes*, Leslie S. Klinger, pp. 1016-1017, fn 13
7. 1861 c.100 (regnal.24 and 25 Vict)
8. Matrimonial Causes Act 1857 (20 & 21 Vict. c. 85)
9. Ibid.
10. There is no statute that can be cited for authority, The action is based solely upon case law.

VOL. LXV
PUCK BUILDING, New York
PRICE TEN CENTS
PUCK
CONGRESS
THE ADVENTURE OF THE CROOKED HOUSE

Crossword Puzzle

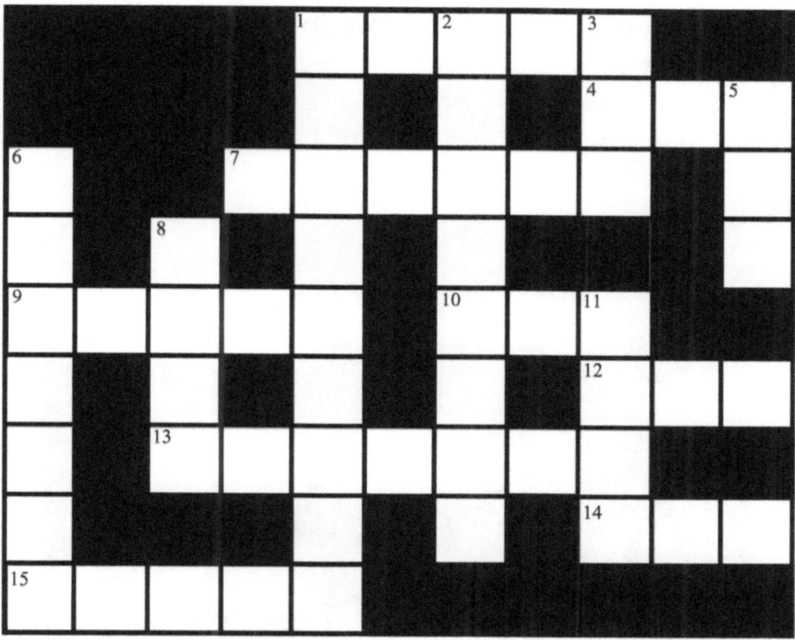

Across

1. The page
4. The sun was over this
7. His Boswell
9. The nationality of the interpreter
10. The large mammal from Sumatra
12. Jabez Wilson bought a penny bottle of ___ for his new job.
13. What happened in Bohemia.
14. The man on the ___ was outlined against the moon.
15. Holmes described Count Sylvius as one of these.

Down

1. The man from Ballarat (two words)
2. A ferret-like Scotland Yarder
3. Hither and ____
5. Jefferson Hope shook this in the face of Enoch Drebber.
6. An Irregular
8. The landlady babbled of green ___.
11. Mary Sutherland wore her hat with a ____.

Crossword Puzzle Answers

				1 B	I	2 L	L	3 Y		
				L		E		4 O	A	5 K
6 W			7 W	A	T	S	O	N		E
I		8 P		C		T				Y
9 G	R	E	E	K		10 R	A	11 T		
G		A		J		A		12 I	N	K
I		13 S	C	A	N	D	A	L		
N				C		E		14 T	O	R
15 S	H	A	R	K						

The Detective in Real Life

by

'Alfred Aylmer'

originally published in

The Windsor Magazine Vol. 1 page 499

[Editor's note: The original British spelling has been retained in this article. In addition, there are some words and phrases in French which are explained when they are not obvious. The author's name was published in quotes which suggests it was a pseudonym. Some people believe it was written by Arthur Griffiths who wrote a number of books and essays about police and crime. Project Gutenberg has some of Arthur Griffiths' books available online.]

Since Edgar Allan Poe first invented "Dupin" and the analytic method of solving criminal mysteries, the detective, both professional and amateur, has been a prominent personage in fiction and on the stage. He has been made the central figure of innumerable novels and plays; he is often the hero and protagonist, the pivot on which the plot hangs. He may be the chorus, but more often he is the god from the machine, the agent impassive and impartial of avenging fate.

He is always a favourite with reader and audience, whether he is called Hawkshaw, or Captain Redwood, Grice, Stanhope, Van Vernet, Père Tabaret, or Monsieur Lecocq. There were numbers who mourned the tragic death of Sherlock Holmes as though they had lost a dear friend, and now a fresh and nearly as keen an interest is being arousal in "Martin Hewitt, Investigator," the latest, quite one of the best, creations of the kind.

Yet it may be doubted whether imagination has outdone reality, whether fiction is equal to fact, whether the ideal is as interesting or even accurately resembles the real detective officer. No detective stories are stranger than the personal records and reminiscences of the men themselves.

Vidocq's astounding adventures, the memoirs of Canler, Claude, and Macé are less high coloured, but more impressive than any detective romances. The same superiority may be claimed for authentic portraiture as compared with the many imaginary characters so freely invented of late. A picture taken from life cannot but possess a certain truthfulness. It may possibly caricature, exaggerate, even mislead—so do photographs; but they are still the real thing, not fancy-drawn sketches, and must exhibit some actual phase in the aspect of the sitter.

As I have come across a good many detectives from time to time, both in public and in private, on official business and in private intercourse, I propose to set down some account of them as I have known them and seen them at work. It may be necessary to speak of some under pseudonyms; where they are still serving it might not be always discreet to mention the real name. The same reserve need not apply to those who have gone over to the majority or retired from active duty.

This latter is the condition of M. Macé, the former well-known head of the Parisian *police de la sûreté*, or detective police of Paris. M. Macé achieved some sensational and extraordinary triumphs in detection, and his first, when still but a police commissary in one of the out quarters, gave an earnest of his future usefulness.

It was in the case of the murder of an old man named Linotte, who lived alone and was not actually missed until the discovery of certain dismembered limbs aroused suspicion. M. Macé, on forcing an entrance to his rooms, saw at once that although uninhabited they were visited daily, because a cuckoo clock was going, and it was a clock that must be wound up every twenty-four hours. Later in the inquiry he localised the spot where the murder and dismemberment had taken place by emptying a decanter on the floor and finding that it gradually dried everywhere except in one place, which was still damp with the blood effused by the victim.

It was my good fortune to be thrown a good deal with M. Macé once, and I remember him and some of his methods well. In appearance he was a small, fair man, with a mild, thoughtful eye, a soft voice, and a gentle, unassuming, and yet persuasive manner. He might have been an inventor or a mathematician, possibly a schoolmaster, for he was a little pedantic, and liked to put one right with one's French whenever idiom or pronunciation went astray. His favourite costume was the decorous suit of black and the white tie of the French officer of justice. There were times when he assumed disguise, and he could do it with the best, but disguises are much less used by detectives than is commonly supposed. There have been several successors to M. Macé, but none have outshone him in detection. M. Goron, who till quite recently occupied the post, was a man of a different type, more showy, perhaps, a rapid talker, fond of gesture and of dramatic effect. M. Goron did excellent service in his time, especially against the Anarchists, but he has now left the Prefecture, and resumed the duties of a police commissary.

M. Macé was an indefatigable worker; at his office—in those days, in a corner of the Palais de Justice—early and late, coming generally at 7 a.m., and remaining often till 10, 11, even 12 o'clock at night, unless he was called away, for it is the rule in Paris when any great crime has been committed to summon the *chef de la sûreté* without delay, and the chief himself, for obvious reasons, is anxious to be early upon the scene of the catastrophe.

But otherwise he seldom left the Palais except to go home, where he always took his meals— as a rule a short hour for breakfast and the same for dinner sufficed; he was a very domestic little man, loved the *coin du feu* [by the fireside]. Even there he was within easy reach of the Prefecture, and was ready to go round at any hour, day or night, whenever he was sent for

I have sat with M. Macé through the day in his little bureau, hung round with relics and reminiscences of crimes, the sort of thing to be seen any day at the Black Museum in Scotland Yard.

His first business was the simple routine duties, inspecting "states," reading the return of any arrests made during the previous twenty-four hours. Then he scanned the whole of the morning papers for items of police news; where the reporters went too far he liked to put them right, where they were still in the dark he found it convenient sometimes to enlighten. Every afternoon, with this idea, he gave an interview to pressmen; it paid him well to furnish his own account of whatever was going on. The morning's correspondence was next disposed of; a lengthy affair, for all manner of people write to the *chef de la sûreté* seeking his advice or intervention, sometimes offering it to assist in the detection of still undiscovered crimes.

Every country has its amateur detectives, and very officious and wearisome they sometimes prove to the professional police officer. That is sufficiently well known to our own police officers, who were in undated with suggestions for the capture of Jack the Ripper. Only a few months back a most elaborate scheme was put forward by some silly busybody for proving Read's innocence, and discovering the real perpetrator of the Southend murder.

Then came M. Macé's morning *levée.* [A time when a government official is approachable.] There were many waiting for interviews, but they had not to wait long, nor when once admitted were they suffered to waste much of his time. I sat with him through one of these *levées*, and greatly admired the tact and promptitude with which he despatched the morning's business.

First, a mother and son appeared. They had been haggling over a sum of money, the proceeds of a small inheritance which they ought to have divided; now they came to say they have so agreed. "*Ça tranche la question,*"[That settles the matter.] the incident was ended, "Good morning."

Now a sub., the confidential clerk, a foxy-haired youth with weak eyes, brings up a small brown paper parcel. "One moment, please," says M. Macé as he deftly loosens the strings. Inside was a shirt, the missing link in a chain, Macé declares, on finding it marked with certain initials. "Put it with the other *pièces à conviction* [evidence]; that completes the evidence. What next?"

A prisoner who has been caught red-handed about day dawn in an *appartement* not his own, and with stolen property on him. He is a respectable, harmless-looking youth.

"And what makes you a thief?" the *chef* asked him sharply. "You cannot be in want?"

The lad, who is in good clothes, and carries a shiny hat, hangs his head.

"Well, how did you get it?" proceeds the interrogator. "By force?"

"No, with a false key."

"Of what kind?" and M. Macé points to a series of photographs on the walls, representing all known varieties of false keys.

"That," answers the accused, pointing, without hesitation.

The key itself was in the hands of the police; why try to withhold information?

"Who else was in the job?"

"No one."

"Bah. What is your trade or calling? Been convicted before? Where, when, for what?

Sentence—six months? Father alive?"

"Yes."

"Mother?"

"No—stepmother. Madame La Bellemere is outside."

"Well, let her come in."

A lady, or a very good imitation of one, well but showily dressed, entered. She was overwhelmed with grief, and began at once to upbraid her stepson, whom she sees now for the first time since his arrest. Then she attacked the chef, imploring his clemency.

"The lad is not really *méchant*; he means well; he has been led into this by evil associates; he is a good honest youth."

"And yet he has a previous conviction against him, madame."

"True," she replied, a little disconcerted, "but he was a victim then, as now."

"What is his trade?"

"He's a —"

"Typographe," the youth interposed hurriedly, evidently afraid his stepmother might make some mistake.

"Indeed?" the chef said drily, as he caught at the lad's hand and examined his thumb and forefinger.

They were black, but with tobacco juice, not printer's ink.

"I must know who else was in this," insisted the stern official. "Take him away."

"Now, Madame," he went on, when the accused had been removed, "will you tell me who were the other parties?"

Instead of replying frankly, she had recourse to a woman's weapons–tears and entreaties, declaring that they are people of good position, respected in their quarter, that they will be overwhelmed with shame and disgrace by the scandal of this thing.

"That's all very likely," said M. Macé coldly, "but I am an official functionary; I have to deal with justice, not with family affairs," and he was about to bow her out. "If I only knew who—" he added tentatively, with his hand on the door-knob, "If I only knew who else was in the robbery, your stepson might get off."

"I can tell you," she now cried excitedly.

"Ah! A woman, no doubt? A bad woman? I was sure of it. And her name is — "

"I cannot quite remember, but she lives, or is to be heard of, at the Brasserie Cochin Chine, Rue des Carroubleurs. I will find out exactly, and I will come again. Meanwhile, you will take every care of my poor boy?"

"Of that you may rest assured," replied the *chef* with a meaning smile; and presently the youth is marched off to the prison of detention at Mazas.

A gentleman well dressed, well-to-do, was the next caller; he is a little nervous and shamefaced, perhaps, but nothing of the criminal about him. He had had the misfortune to lose a large sum in bank notes—fifty thousand francs worth. He had dropped them, left them behind him, forgotten them. Where? Somewhere, anywhere—he could not remember. He is rather incoherent; his story is confused and contradictory. When questioned his statements vary, all but the one fact of his loss.

"They were not stolen, I suppose?" the chef asked with a keen look.

"I cannot say; I think I dropped them."

"Where and how did you carry them?"

"In my breast pocket."

"In a purse?"

"No, wrapped in a parcel, in paper— newspaper."

"Really! Fifty thousand francs in a piece of old newspaper— extraordinary!"

"You do not disbelieve my story, I suppose?" the applicant exclaimed with some indignation.

"Certainly not; Monsieur's assertion is more than sufficient.

Still—" M. Macé gave a significant glance towards the pile of papers on the table. Just then there were two loud knocks in succession at the door—a plain hint that other visitors were growing impatient.

"At least, tell me what I had better do."

"Advertise. Put it about. Say when and where you had the notes last. Offer an ample reward."

The poor man went off, and the chef turned to me muttering significantly, "*Mauvais lieux,*" [bad places] a plain hint as to his notion when and where the notes had disappeared.

But his easily aroused professional suspicion was in this case misplaced, as the sequel showed. The notes, still in their strange cover, were actually dropped upon the grand Boulevards. The bulky parcel attracted the notice of three young soldiers, who made a football of it for some hundreds of yards along the pavements. Then one of them picked it up and secreted it unobserved in a comrade's haversack. The unconscious possessor of two thousand pounds was on his way home on a short furlough, and did not open his haversack, but on reaching his father's cottage at Neuilly threw it on a shelf. There it lay unnoticed for several days; at length it was opened by one of the family and the treasure revealed. They were honest folk, these French peasants, and they were anxious to restore the money to its rightful owners. So they went to the nearest official—a brigadier of gendarmes—who examined the notes.

He found on one of them the name of a Parisian broker, to whom he at once telegraphed.

The story of the lost notes had been mentioned in the papers, and the news of their recovery was quickly communicated to the loser, who hastened to Neuilly by the first train. It is but fair to add that he gave the peasants a handsome reward.

Not the least important part of the French detective's duties is the preparation of cases for his *juge d'instruction*, the stern official who interrogates every accused person, and it is to be feared generally considers a man guilty until he can prove his innocence. The *chef de la sureté* has therefore, access to all accused, and visits them regularly in prison, just in a friendly way to talk over the whole affair. I went with M. Macé one Monday to Mazas and accompanied him to several cells. We stayed longest with a suspected murderer—who was afterwards executed — but against whom there was nothing but circumstantial evidence. The judge had plied him hard to obtain a confession, or at least admissions, but without success. Now M. Macé came with one of his skilful assistants to have a chat. Chairs were placed for us in the cell, the prisoner was requested with much courtesy to be seated, the chef brought out his cigar case, which was handed round, and we all settled down quite good friends.

The detective agent—let me call him Adhemar—was a curious creature: a great, big, portly man, in a responsible – looking frock coat, in which was the red ribbon, his hat was as broad brimmed as a Quaker's, but very curly. He was coarse-featured, with a long nose, very dark, sallow skin, and dull, stagnant eyes, but the most jovial, open-hearted manner possible. He had, as M. Macé said, *l'air si bonasse* [a good natured air]. He seemed such a simpleton, in fact, that no one could have imagined he was playing a part. But he was acting all through; did all the talking, and in the most dramatic way proceeded to tell Gilles exactly how he had committed the crime.

"You had often seen the old lady. You knew she had economies; where she kept the magot (property); you watched your opportunity, frequently passing to and fro up and down the street"—Adhemar stealthily paced the cell. "One evening she was alone in the kitchen, stirring the *pot au feu* [a French dish of boiled beef and vegetables]; her back was towards you; you crept up to her"— Adhemar acted the stealthy movement across the cell. "You stood behind her thus; you raised your hand, armed with a cleaver, and struck down with all your force, cric–crac—she fell dead—hein? Wasn't that it, eh?"

Adhemar turned suddenly on Gilles to see the effect of his words, hoping that he had worked him up to the last pitch of excitement and that surely he would let some unguarded expression escape. We were watching Gilles closely, and once, as though the scene was again before him, I saw a flash in his eye, the first symptom of a shiver, a start involuntary, but immediately suppressed. By the time Adhemar turned — the prisoner had recovered his self-possession, now he only shook his head and smiled vaguely. He was not to be caught that day.

There were many trusted subordinates then as now, who were ready to face any discomfort, run any risks, to compass an arrest. While we were patiently going the rounds of the night-houses and were seeking suicide by trying the villainous brandy cherries at the drink shop of the once notorious *Père Lunettes*, once one of the lowest and vilest haunts in Paris, a man in a blue blouse and a flat silk cap, a *voyou* [thug] of the most forbidding aspect, came up and fraternised, even to the extent of following us into the street, importuning. My conductor, one of M. Macé's chief assistants, laughed afterwards when we broke away.

"He does it well. That is our Jules; he will go far. He has been here in this *bouge*,[sleazy place] this infamous quarter, three weeks —it is an intricate case—but he is on the brink of something interesting."

I asked if this was often done.

"It is most necessary at times," replied my informant. He was an old soldier, Bertrand by name, who still retained the erect military carriage and was always punctiliously neat in his appearance. Yet he once went through all the inconvenience of a fortnight's imprisonment, and associated with a well-known ruffian who had a secret which he wished to worm out of him.

"How did you like it?" I inquired.

"Not much. I could not stomach the food; my cell companion, however, disposed of most of that. The deprivation of tobacco, too, was awful, only I sometimes got a whiff at the reception when I went down to have a short talk with the instructing judge. The chief warder managed that for me. He was the only one in the secret, and stood by me when the ward officer wished to force me to go to exercise in the general yard. Why there were dozens of prisoners there who would have known me by sight."

"And did you find out what you wanted?"

"Yes, yes. He confided the whole secret to me. You should have seen his face when I was put into the box to give evidence. He had still stoutly denied the one fact to which I could now swear. Although he was taken aback when taxed with it he still would admit nothing. But when the presiding judge asked me my name and quality, and I replied 'Bertrand, *inspecteur de la police de sureté de Paris*, it was all over. 'I chuck—it's no good,' and he made a clean breast of the whole thing."

No doubt the French police employ methods that may seem a little underhand, but their defence is that they are acting in the best interests of justice. Our own police are not above similar subterfuges.

It is an old story now how a once famous inspector in his time secured the arrest of Tarpey, the jewel robber. It was through making desperate love to Tarpey's wife.

A detective, whom I will not name, as he afterwards came to conspicuous grief, admitted to me that he would never have succeeded in a certain case but for stealing a letter. He wanted an address, and had strong reasons for suspecting it was contained in a letter he saw the postman deliver at a house he was watching. By some plausible story he got possession of this letter, which he opened without scruple, and obtained the address. When the man wanted was at last arrested, and charged before a magistrate, the detective very prudently declined to say how he had obtained the address.

The English detective officer is perhaps more familiar to us than the French. Most of us have met or had to do with them in some way or other, yet few probably know them really. The late estimable Mr. Williamson, who spent a lifetime at Scotland Yard, and was long the life and soul of the detective department, starting as private and ending as chief constable, was little more than a name to the public through all his long years of arduous and uncompromising service.

Few but the initiated recognised in this quiet, unpretending, middle-sized man, who walked leisurely along Whitehall, balancing a hat, that was a little large for him, loosely on his head, and often with a sprig of a leaf or flower between his lips, was the redoubtable detective. He was naturally very reticent; no outsider could win

from him any details of the many big things he had put through. His talk, for choice, was about gardening, for which he had a perfect passion; and his blooms were famous in the neighbourhood where he spent his unofficial hours. Another very favourite diversion with him, until the increasing pressure of work denied him any leisure, was boating. He was very much at home on the Thames, a powerful sculler, and very fond of it. He never missed till the very last a single Oxford and Cambridge boat race, seeing it for choice from the police steam launch—the very best way indeed of going to the race, but a pleasure reserved for the Home Secretary, police officials, and a few of their most intimate friends. The police-boat is the last to go down the course and the first to follow the competing eights.

One or two especially trying circumstances helped to break Williamson down rather prematurely. He took very much to heart the misconduct of certain detectives in the once well-known and notorious de Goncourt turf frauds. He was at that time practically the head of his branch, and some of the blame—but, of course, none of the disgrace—was visited upon him, as it was argued that his subordinates had been allowed too free a hand. This may have been the case; but he had to deal with men of uncommon astuteness, who were the more unscrupulous because he trusted them so implicitly, with the trust of a right loyal nature, true to those above him, and counting upon the same from his subordinates. Meiklejohn, a shrewd Scotchman—persistent, untiring—was clever enough for anything; he had made many notable arrests before he came to grief, and he was excessively lucky—one of the chief merits in a detective, as I have heard the best of them often say.

On one occasion, for instance, Meiklejohn was following a clue when he met a comparative stranger, asked a simple question, was struck by the reply, turned and shadowed the man, and was led straight into the solution of the criminal problem he had in hand.

Mr. Williamson's active career was also chequered by the nature of the crimes which kept him most busily employed. Fenianism might have been found written on his heart, like Calais on Queen Mary's, and closely interwoven with it Anarchism and Nihilism in all their phases.

He knew no peace when foreign potentates were the guests of our royalties; Scotland Yard was, in fact, held responsible for the safety of Czar and Emperor, and the police authorities depended principally on Williamson, with his consummate knowledge and long experience in exotic crime.

It was Williamson who was first on the scene when dynamite was discovered, infernal machines had exploded, or might be expected to do so at any moment.

To him the officer who is nowadays our chief mainstay and defence against these outrages, Inspector Melville, owes much of his insight into the peculiar business of the "special section," as this important branch of criminal investigation is called.

The latter not long ago disposed very ingeniously of a case which might have led to very serious mischief. Fertility of resource with great promptitude in action are among Mr. Melville's strongest and most valuable traits. On one occasion, during the visit to England of a foreign Sovereign, information was received that one of his subjects residing in this country, and by no means loyal to him, intended to do him an injury the first time he could get near him in public. It so happened that at that moment the Emperor was on the point of joining in a great procession, which had either actually started or would in the course of an hour or so. The malcontent was employed as cellarman to a wine and spirit merchant or publican with large wine vaults. There was no time to lose, and Melville made the best of his way to the place, saw the proprietor, and enquired for a certain brand of champagne he wished to purchase. The master called his man and sent them down together into the cellars. The cellarman went first with a light; at the bottom of the staircase he unlocked the wine cellar and went in—still first.

"What wine is that over yonder?" asked Melville carelessly, and the man crossed over to the far end of the vault to look before he answered. This was all the astute officer wanted. With a sudden inspiration he seized upon the opportunity, stepped back out of the cellar, closed the door promptly and locked it. The irreconcileable cellarman was a prisoner, and was left there perfectly unable to carry out his fell purpose. After the procession was over he was set free.

Most of the prominent detectives of today learnt their work under Williamson—Butcher, now chief inspector, who is as fond of flowers as his master, and may be known by the fine rose in his buttonhole; Littlechild, who earned his first reputation in unravelling and exposing Long Firm and assurance office frauds; Neald, the present curator of the Black Museum, a sturdy, self-reliant, solid detective officer, with the esprit of his calling strong in him, who, among other great cases, worked to a successful issue the "Orrock" murder, when the syllable "rock" scratched upon a chisel led to ultimate detection.

The exposure of the detectives' misdeeds in 1876 brought a superior official to Scotland Yard, and the first head of the newly named Criminal Investigation Department was Colonel Howard Vincent.

His appointment was a surprise to many, and his fitness for the post was not immediately apparent. He was young, comparatively speaking, unknown in experienced police matters, with no previous record but a brief military service, followed by a call to the bar. But he was energetic, painstaking, a man of order, with some power of organisation; above all, a gentleman of high character and integrity. His reign at Whitehall Place might not have been marked by any phenomenal feats in detection; in the pursuit of crime he was dependent upon his most able subordinates, and it was his rule to summon the most experienced to advise on all serious cases.

In the more subtle processes of analysis and deduction, of working from effect to cause, from vague almost impalpable indices to strong presumption of guilt, Howard Vincent did not shine; he did not always realise the value of reticence and secrecy in detective operations; but he did good work at Scotland Yard by raising the general tone and systematising the service.

Mr. Anderson, the Assistant Commissioner of Police, the present chief of the Investigation Department, is an ideal detective officer, with a natural bias for the work, and endowed with gifts peculiarly useful in it. He is a man of the quickest apprehension, with the power of close, rapid reasoning from facts, suggestions, or even impressions. He seizes on the essential point almost by intuition, and is marvellously ready in finding the real clue or indicating the right trail. With all this he is the most discreet, the most silent and reserved of public functionaries. Someone said he was a mystery even to himself. This to him inestimable quality of reticence is not unaided by a slight but perhaps convenient deafness, which Mr. Anderson cultivates and parades on occasions. If he is asked an embarrassing question, he quickly puts up his hand and says the enquiry has been addressed to his deaf ear. But I shrewdly suspect he

hears all that he wishes to hear; little goes on around him that is not noted and understood; without seeming to pay much attention, he is always listening and drawing his own conclusions.

Subordinates naturally look up to such a leader, relying confidently upon his advice, and eager for his encouragement. Of course he holds his whole department in the hollow of his hand; from his desk he can communicate with all its branches. The speaking tubes hang just behind his chair. A little further off is the office telephone, which brings him into converse with Sir Edward Bradford, the Chief Commissioner, or colleagues and subordinates in more distant parts of the house. He is, and must be, perforce, an indefatigable worker, for the labours of his department are unceasing, and often of the most anxious, even disappointing, character.

THE ILLUSTRATED POLICE NEWS
LAW COURTS AND WEEKLY RECORD

Although he has achieved greater success than any detective of his time, there will always be undiscovered crimes, and just now the tale is pretty full. Much dissatisfaction was vented upon Mr. Anderson at the utterly abortive efforts to discover the perpetrator of the Whitechapel murders. He has himself a perfectly plausible theory that Jack the Ripper was a homicidal maniac, temporarily at large, whose hideous career was cut short by committal to an asylum.

Mr. Macnaghten, the Chief Constable, or second in command of the Investigation Department, is a type of man admirably adapted to supplement his chief. He is essentially a man of action, while Mr. Anderson is perhaps best and strongest in the closet. He is in very close touch, too, with the personnel of the department, who gladly recognise his authority, and are eager to second him and give effect to his views. A man of presence is Mr. Macnaghten, tall, well-built, with a military air, although his antecedents are rather those of the public school, of Indian planter life, and not of the army. His room, like his chief's, is hung with speaking tubes, his table deep with reports and papers, but the walls are bright with photographs of officials, personal friends, and of some notorious criminals.

If you can persuade Mr. Macnaghten, he will show you some other and more gruesome pictures, which are carefully kept under lock and key; photographs, for instance, of the victims of Jack the Ripper and of other brutal murders, taken immediately after discovery, and reproducing with horrible fidelity the mutilated remains of a human body, but which might belong to a charnel house or abattoir. It is Mr. Macnaghten's duty, no less than his earnest desire, to be first on the scene of any such sinister catastrophe. He is therefore more intimately acquainted perhaps with the details of the most recent celebrated crimes than anyone in Scotland Yard.

Under such chiefs as these the rank and file labour, assiduously utilising the qualities which really serve them best, patience and persistence, following the hints and suggestions given them by their more thoughtful leaders. The best detective is he who has that infinite capacity for taking trouble, which has been defined as the true test of genius. It is not by guesses or sensational snap-shots that crimes are unearthed, but by the slow process of routine, almost common place enquiry, after the most minute painstaking investigation of the traces left upon the theatre of the deed. The smallest clues, in the hands of these laborious workers, will often bring them to the end of the labyrinth.

THE ILLUSTRATED POLICE NEWS
LAW COURTS AND WEEKLY RECORD

Not long ago half a horn button picked up on the floor of a house rifled by burglars led to the arrest of the perpetrators.

The detective employed remembered that certain notorious "family men" were just then at large, and he made it his business to beat up their quarters. Fortune, that still most useful adjunct in detection, helped him, for the man he wanted was in custody for some minor offence, and he was discovered in a police cell wearing the very coat with the other half of the broken button.

When the pursuit was hottest after the French anarchist, François, the trail was lost by his sudden change of residence. But someone in the locality he last lived in remembered the name on the van by which his goods were removed. This led the detectives employed to hunt up every van proprietor in London till they found the man they wanted. In the old days M. Canler, the famous French detective, "ran in "a murderer who had dropped a piece of paper supplied by a butterman; he made it his business to visit every butterman's shop in Paris, and eventually succeeded in his purpose.

Some of our best private inquiry agents have been trained in this way, their instincts developed, their methods systematised by the discipline and experience of regular police work. The private detective is a peculiar product of our latter-day civilisation, called into being by the complexity of modern life. It would take too long to trace here the causes which led to his creation—the reasons, some not too worthy or easily defensible, which impel people to set a watch upon each other, to unearth past histories, spy out present proceedings. But the unofficial, yet still professional, investigation is often the foreshadower and forerunner of legal process. Thus the recent unsavoury case which has disgusted society and shattered some reputations was entirely prepared by an ex-inspector of Scotland Yard, the Mr. Littlechild already mentioned as a former light of the department. Another well-known agent, Mr. Andrews, also learnt his business in the Metropolitan Police, and he has had the conduct of more than one preliminary preparation of a *cause célèbre*. Like Littlechild, he is an excellent specimen of his class: discreet, untiring, full of resource.

To me the most amusing result of my long acquaintance with detectives is the opportunity it gives me of often recognizing them in strange places at unexpected times. I have come across them travelling in trains, on board steamboats, at hotels, always on the alert, of course, but betraying nothing in ways or appearance of their interesting profession. I have watched with peculiar pleasure the detectives kept in "the rooms" by the "administration" of the Monte Carlo Casino, especially when they ran in some notorious *escroc* [swindler], or sharper, whom they had long been shadowing. I have given my coat and hat to a detective at a great London reception in a historic house where many of the guests were titled or celebrated people, but into which others, unbidden and extremely undesirable, had been known to insinuate themselves in the prosecution of their nefarious trade. I have met detectives at a wedding breakfast, at a light dinner, at balls during the season, and I can safely assert that these "professionals." were certainly not the least gentlemanlike in manners or costumes of the guests assembled.

One or two anecdotal stories of the ingenuity, the patient pertinacity, the determination to succeed so often displayed by the private inquiry agent may fitly end this article. I knew one who was employed by a famous firm of solicitors in a very delicate operation, which he terminated successfully, but in a way to show that he did not stick at trifles in securing his end. It was the sequel to a divorce case. The decree nisi had been granted, and against the wife, who had been refused the custody of the one child born of the marriage. The husband was anxious to secure possession of the child, but the ex-wife, like so many more of her sex, was much too sharp to be forestalled. She had a friend waiting at the court who, directly the decree was pronounced, started off in a hansom to the lady's residence, where the child was, laid hands on it, and brought it down to Victoria Station just in time for the night mail to the Continent, by which lady and child travelled together to the south of France. A detective was at once despatched in pursuit by the husband's lawyer, and his orders were at all costs to recover possession of the child.

He soon got upon the lady's track. She had not gone further than Monte Carlo. The detective found it impossible to kidnap the child, so he managed to make friends with the mother, gradually grew very intimate, paid her devoted attention, and eventually married her. When he was her husband he had no difficulty in completing his commission, and – possibly with the lady's full consent—he soon sent the child home. I never heard how this marriage— all in the way of business—turned out.

Another story is, perhaps, more dramatic. A man of considerable property, strictly entailed, who was married, died childless in India. The estates went to the next of kin, but he, just as he was entering into their enjoyment, was startled by a telegram from his relative's widow preparing him for the birth of a posthumous child. He at once consulted his lawyer, who, after warning him that much time and money would probably be spent in the process, promised to expose the fraud, if fraud there was, or, at any rate, prove that it was a bond fide affair.

A year passed, and yet the next of kin had heard nothing of the case. At last he went to his lawyers and insisted upon knowing how it stood. He was told that the matter was now ripe; the lady had arrived with her infant son. She was actually at that moment at a private hotel in the West End.

"Go and call on her, and insist upon seeing the child. If there's any difficulty about it, go out on the landing and call out 'Bartlett!' A man will come down and explain everything."

The lady did not produce the child when asked; she said it was out in the park with its nurse, and tried all sorts of excuses, so Bartlett was summoned.

"I want to see the child," says the next of kin.

"This lady's? She has no child. I have been with her now for six months, and she has asked me repeatedly to get her one—anywhere, in Cairo, at the Foundling in Malta, here in London."

"Who are you, then?" both inquired, astonished beyond measure.

And "Bartlett," having completed his mission, quietly informed the lady, whom he had been watching, and the next of kin, who was really his employer, that he was the detective engaged to unravel the case.

With such men as this long-continued fraud, however astutely prepared, becomes almost impossible. The private inquiry agent is generally equal to any emergency.

I can remember another story—it shall be the last—of a detective, crossing on a Channel steamer to France, when he ran up against the very person he was intended to watch in Paris. It was of the utmost importance that this person should not realise the detective's mission, who, by the way was perfectly well known to him. Before the steamer reached Calais the detective had persuaded the other to give him a job in Paris, as though he had had no idea of going there, a job which would enable him, moreover, to carry out all the better the original mission on which he had been dispatched.

"Lodging-Houses"

Chapter Seven of

London's Underworld

by

Thomas Holmes

First published in 1912

Currently in the Public Domain

[Editor's Note: Copies of the book, *London's Underworld,* can be found in print and online. The writing is sometimes insightful and compassionate, and sometimes harsh and paternalistic. Punctuation and spelling are as they were in the original.]

The inmates of the underworld lodging-houses are a queer and heterogeneous lot; but they are much to be preferred to the sleepers out; because rascally though many of them are, there is a good deal of self-reliance and not a little enterprise amongst them. By hook and crook, and, it is to be feared, mostly by crook, they obtain sufficient money for food and lodging, and to this extent they are an improvement upon the sleepers out. They have, too, some pluck, perseverance and talents that, rightly applied, might be of considerable benefit to the community. But having got habituated to the liberty of common lodging-houses, and to the excitement of getting day by day just enough for each day's need, though sometimes fasting and sometimes feasting, the desire for settled home life and for the duties of citizenship has vanished. For with the money to pay night by night for their lodgings, responsibility to rent and tax collector ends.

I must allow some exceptions, for once every year there comes upon thousands of them the burden of finding five shillings to pay for the hawker's licence that provides them with the semblance of a living or an excuse for begging. After much experience of this class, including many visits to common lodging-houses, and some friendships with the inmates, I am sure that the desire to be untrammelled with and municipal obligation leads a great percentage of the occupants prefer the life to any other. They represent to some extent in modern and industrial age the descendants of Jonadab, the son Rechab, with this exception, they arc by no means averse to the winecup. It is to be feared that there is a growth in this portion of our community, for every scheme for providing decent lodgings for homeless men is eagerly taken advantage of by men who might and who ought to live in homes of their own, and so fulfil the duties of decent citizenship

In this respect even Lord Rowton's estimable lodging-houses and those, too, of our municipal authorities prove no exception for they attract numbers of men who ought not to be there, but who might, with just a little more self-reliance and self-respect, live comfortably outside.

I pass on to the common lodging-houses that accommodate a lower class than is found in municipal or Rowton houses. Probably none or at any rate very few, of my readers have had a practical experience of common lodging-houses. I have, so therefore I ask them to accompany me to one of them.

In a dingy slum stand a number of grimy houses that have been converted into one big house. The various doorways have been blocked and one enlarged entrance serves.

As we enter, the money-taker in his office demands our business. We tell him that we are anxious to have a look round, and he tells us he will send for the deputy. The deputy is the autocrat governs sway in this domain of semi-darkness and dirt. We stand aside in the half-lit passage, taking good care that we have no contact with the walls; the air we breathe is thick with unpleasant odours and we realise at once, and to our complete satisfaction, the smell and flavour of a common lodging-house. We know instinctively that we have made its acquaintance before, it seems familiar to us, but we are puzzled about it until we remember we have had a foretaste of it given to us by some lodging-house habitues that we met. The aroma of a common lodging-house cannot be concealed, it is not to be mistaken.

It is six o'clock p.m., the days are short, for it is November. The lodgers are arriving, so we stand and watch them as they pass the little office and pay their sixpences. Down goes the money, promptly a numbered ticket takes its place; few words are exchanged, and away go the ticket-holders to the general kitchen.

Presently the deputy comes to interview us, and he does not put us at ease; he is a forbidding fellow, one that evidently will stand no nonsense. Observe, if you please, that he has lost his right hand, and that a formidable iron hook replaces it. Many a time has that hook been serviceable; if it could speak, many tales would it tell of victories won, of rows quelled, and of blood spilled.

We have seen the fellow previously, and more than once, at local police~court. Sometimes he came as prosecutor, sometimes

prisoner, and at other times as witness. When the police had required to supplement the power of his iron hand in the many free fights, he appeared sometimes in the dual capacity prisoner and prosecutor.

We know that he retains his position because of his strength the unscrupulous way in which he uses it. He knows us too, but he is not well pleased to see us! Nevertheless, he accedes to our request "just a look round." So through a large passage we pass, and he ushers us into the lodging-house kitchen. As the door opens a babel voices greets us, a rush of warm air comes at us, and the evidence our noses proclaims that bloaters and bacon, liver and onions, sausages and fresh fish are being cooked. We look and see, we see and taste! Strange eyes are turned upon us just for a moment, but we not "'tecs," so the eyes are turned back to the different frying-pans or roasting-forks, as the case may be. See how they crowd round the huge and open fire, for there is no cooking range. See how they elbow other as they want space for this pan or that fork. See how the bloaters curl and twist as if trying to escape from the forks and the fire. See how the sausages burst and splutter in their different pans. See how stolidly the tough steaks brown, refusing either to splutter, yield fat, find gravy to assist in their own undoing.

Listen to the sizzling that pervades the place, acting as an orchestral accompaniment to the chorus of human voices. Listen to it all, breathe it all, let your noses and your ears take it all in. Then let your eyes and your imagination have their turn before the pungency of rank tobacco adds to the difficulty of seeing and breathing. And so we look, and we find there are sixty human beings of both sexes and various ages in that kitchen. Some of them we know, for have we not seen them in Cheapside, St. Paul's Churchyard, or elsewhere acting as gutter merchants. Yonder sit an old couple that we have seen selling matches or laces for many years past! It is not a race day, and there being no "test match" or exciting football match, a youth of sixteen earns a precarious living by selling papers in the streets sits beside them. Today papers are at a discount, so he has given up business for the day and sought warmth and company in his favourite lodging house.

Ah! there is our old friend, the street ventriloquist! You see the back of his hand is painted in vivid colours to resemble the face of an old woman. We know that he has a bundle that contains caps and dresses and skirts that will convert his hand and arm into a quaint human figure. Many a droll story can he tell, for he has "padded the hoof" from one end of England to the other; he knows every lodging-house from Newcastle-on-Tyne to Plymouth. He is a graceless dog, fond of a joke, a laugh and a story; he is honest enough and intelligent enough for anything. But of regular life, discipline and work he will have none. By and by, after the cooking is all done, he will want to give a performance and take up a collection.

There are a couple, male and female, who tramp the country lanes; the farm haystacks or outbuildings have been their resting-places during the summer, but approaching winter has sent them back to London.

You see that they have got a tattered copy of Moody and Sankey's hymns which is their stock-in-trade. They have at different lodging-house "services" picked up some slight knowledge of a limited number of tunes, now they are trying to commit the words to memory.

Tomorrow they will in quiet streets be whining out "Oh, where is my boy to-night?" or "Will you meet me at the Fountain?"

Look again—here is a shabby-genteel man who lives by his wits. He is fairly educated and can write a plausible letter. He is dangerous; his stock-in-trade comprises local directories, WHO'S

WHO, annual reports of charitable societies, clergymen's lists, etc., He is a begging-letter writer, and moves from lodging-house to lodging-house; he writes letters for many of the inmates who have some particular tale of woe, or some urgent appeal to make, and he receives a major part of the resultant charity.

He is drunken and bestial. He is a parasite of the worst description for he preys alike on the benevolent and upon the poor wretches whose cause he spouses.

He assumes many names, he changes his addresses adroitly, and ticks off very carefully the names and addresses of people he has defrauded. In fact he is so clever and slippery that the police and the Charity Organization Society cannot locate him. So he thrives, of type of many, for every one of London's lodging-houses can provide us with one or more such cunning rogues.

Yonder sits a "wandering boy" about twenty-eight years of age. He is not thriving and he must needs be content with simple bread and cheese. A roll of cheap "pirated" music lies on his knee and proclaims his method of living. His life has its dangers, for he has great difficulty in providing five shillings for his pedlar's license, and he runs great risk of having his stock seized by the police, and being committed to prison for a fine he cannot pay.

He has brought sorrow and disgrace to his parents, no eye brightens at the mention of his name. Alas! He is a specimen of the "homeless boy" of who is neighbors will sing tomorrow. He is silent and moody, for he is for he is not in funds. Are there none among the company who sheer misfortune has brought down into the underworld? we ask. Aye, there are, for in this kitchen there are representatives of all sorts and conditions. See that man in the corner by himself, speaking to no one, cooking nothing, eating nothing; he is thinking, thinking! This is his first night in a common lodging-house; it is all new to him, he thinks it all so terrible and disgusting.

He seems inclined to run and spend his night in the streets, and perhaps it will be well for him to do so. He looks descent, bewildered and sorrowful; we know at a glance that some misfortune has tripped him up, we see that self-respect is not dead within him. We know that if he stays the night, breathing the foul air, listening to the horrid talk, seeing much and realizing more, feeling himself attacked on all sides by the common pests of common lodging-houses, we know that tomorrow morning his self-respect will be lessened, his moral power weakened, and his hope of social recovery almost gone. Let him stay a few weeks, then the lodging-house will become his home and his joy. So we feel inclined to cry out and warn him to escape with his life. This is the great evil and danger of common lodging-houses; needful as they undoubtedly are for the homeless and the outcast, they place the unfortunate on an inclined plane down which they slide to complete demoralisation.

I am told that there are four hundred large common lodging-houses in London, many of them capable of holding several hundred ledgers, and which night after night are filled with weird collection of humanity. And they cast a fatal spell upon all who get accustomed to them. Few, very few who have become acclimatised ever go back settled home life. For the decencies, amenities and restraints of citizenship become distasteful. And truly there is much excitement in the life for excitement, at any rate, abounds in the common lodging-house.

Nothing happens in them but the unexpected, and that brings its joys and terrors, its laughter and its tears. Here a great deal of unrestrained human nature is given free play, and the results are exciting if not edifying. Let us spend an evening, but not a night — that is too much to ask— with the habitués.

We sit apart and listen to the babel of voices, but we listen in vain for the lodging-house slang of which we are told so much. They speak very much like other people, and speak on subjects upon which other people speak. They get as excited as ordinary people, too.

Yonder is a lewd fellow shouting obscenities to a female, who, in an equally loud voice and quite as unmistakable language, returns him a Roland for every Oliver.

Here are a couple of wordy and excitable fellow who are arguing the pros and cons of Free Trade and Tariff Reform. They will keep at it till the lights are put out, for both are supplied with a plentiful supply of contradictory literature. Both have fluent tongues, equally bitter, and, having their audience, they, like other people, must contend for mastery. Not that they care for the rights or wrongs of either question, for both are prepared, as occasion serves, to take either side. Religion, too, is excitedly discussed, for an animated couple are discussing Christian Evidences, while the ventriloquist gives parsons generally and bishops in particular a very warm time; even the Pope and General Booth do not escape his scurrilous but witty indictments.

Meanwhile the street singers are practising songs, sacred and secular, and our friend the street minstrel produces an old flute and plays an obbligato, whilst the quivering voice of his poor old wife again wants to know the whereabouts of her wandering boy.

There will be a touching scene when they do meet-may I be there! but I hope they will not meet in a common lodging-house. Another street minstrel is practising new tunes upon a mouth-organ wherewith to soften the hearts of a too obdurate public.

What a babel it all makes; now groups of card-players are quarrelsome, for luck has been against some, or cheating has been discovered; blows are exchanged, and blood flows! As the night advances, men and women under the influence of drink arrive. Some are merry, others are quarrelsome, some are moody and lachrymose. The latter become the butt of the former, the noise increases, confusion itself becomes confounded, and we leave to avoid the general MELEE, and to breathe the night air, which we find grateful and reviving. Phew! but it was hot and thick, we don't want to breathe it again. It is astonishing that people get used to it, and like it too! But it leaves its taint upon them, for it permeates their clothing; they carry it about with them, and anyone who gets a whiff of it gets some idea of the breath of a common lodging-house. And its moral breath effect, too! Woe to all that is fresh and fair, young and hopeful, that within its withering influence. Farewell! a long farewell to truth and self-respect, for the hot breath of a common lodging-house will blast those and every other good quality in young people of either sex that inhale it. Its breath comes upon them, and lo! They become foul without and vile within, carrying their moral and physical with them wherever they go.

A moral sepulchre, or rather crematorium, is the common lodging-house for when its work is done, nothing is left but ashes. For the old habitués I am not much concerned, and though generally I hold a brief for old sinners, criminals and convicts, I hold no brief for the old and middle-aged habitues of a common lodging-house.

Can any one call the dead to life? Can any one convert cold flesh into warm pulsing life? Nay, nay! Talk about being turned into a pillar of salt! the common lodging-house can do more and worse than that! It can turn men and women into pillars of moral death, for even the influence of a long term of penal servitude, withering as it is, cannot for one moment be compared with the corrupting effect of common lodging-house house life.

So the old minstrels may go seeking their wandering boy! and the begging-letter writers may go hang!

The human vultures that prey upon the simple and good-natured may if middle-aged, continue in their evil ways. But what of the young people of whom there ought to be hope? What of them? How long are these "lazar houses" to stand with open door waiting to receive, swallow, transform and eject young humanity? But there is money in them, of course there is; there always is money to be made out of sin and misery if the community permits.

Human wreckage pays, and furnishes a bigger profit than more humdrum investments. I am told by an old habitué with whom I have had endless talks and who has taught me much, although he is a graceless rascal, that one man owns eight of these large establishments, and he and his family live in respectability and wealth.

I have no reason to doubt his statement, for these places are mines of wealth, but the owners take precious good care not to live in them. And infinite care that their families do not inhabit them. Some day when we are wise-but wisdom comes so slowly-these things will not be left to private enterprise, for municipalities will provide and own them at no loss to the ratepayers either.

Then decency, though homeless, will have a chance of survival, and moral and physical cleanliness some chance to live, even in a common lodging-house.

Sadly we need a modern St.George who will face and destroy this monstrous dragon with the fiery breath.

Let it not be said that I am unduly hard upon them who from choice or misfortune inhabit these places. From my heart I pity them, but one cannot be blind to the general consequences. And these things must be taken into consideration when efforts are made, as undoubtedly efforts will some day be made, to tackle this question in a reasonable way.

It is high time, too, that the public understood the difficulties that attend any effort to lift lodging-house habitués to a higher form of existence.

I am bold enough to hazard the statement that the number of these people increases year by year, and that no redemptive effort has had the slightest effect in checking the continual increase. As Secretary of the Howard Association, it is my business year by year to make myself acquainted with the criminal statistics, and all matters connected with our prisons. These statistics more than confirm my statement, for they tell us that while drunkenness, brutality, crimes of violence show a steady decrease, vagabondage, sleeping out, begging, etc., show a continual increase as years roll by.

Of course many of them appear again and again in the prison statistics, nevertheless they form a great and terrible army, whose increase bodes ill for dear and fair old England.

Like birds they are migratory, but they pour no sweetness on the morning or evening air. Like locusts they leave a blight behind.

Like famished wolves when winter draws near they seek the habitations of men. Food they must have! There is corn in Egypt!

When gentle spring returns, then heigho! for the country lanes, villages and provincial towns, and as they move from place to place their trail behind them.

And what a trail it is! ask the governors of our local prisons, ask the guardians of any country districts, ask the farmers, aye, and ask the timid women and pretty children, and, my word for it, they will be able to tell you much of these strange beings that returning summer brings unfailingly before them. Their lodging is sometimes the cold hard ground or the haystack, or perchance, if in luck, an outbuilding.

The prisons are their sanatoria, the workhouses their homes of rest, the casual ward their temporary conveniences. But always before them is one objective, for a common lodging-house is open to them its hypnotism draws them on and on.

So on they go, procreating as they go. Carrying desolation with them, leaving desolation behind them. The endurance of these people—I suppose they must be called people—is marvellous and their rate of progression is sometimes astonishing; weary and footsore, maimed, halt or blind they get over the ground at a good uniform pace.

Look at that strange being that has just passed us as we sat on the bank of a country lane; he goes along with slouching gait and halting steps; he has no boots worthy of the name, his tattered trousers, much too long, give us glimpses of his flesh. He wears an old frock-coat that hangs almost to his heels, and a cloth cap, greasy and worn, upon his head. His beard is wild and abundant, and his hair falls upon his shoulders in a way worthy of an artist or poet.

Follow him, but not too closely, and you will find it hard to keep up with him, he knows what he is making for. Neither George Borrow nor Runciman would hold him for a week, for George would want to stop and talk, but this fellow is silent and grim. A lazar house draws him on, and he needs must reach it, weak and ill-fed though he is! And he will reach others too, for he is on a circular tour. But next winter will find him in a Westminster lodging-house if he has luck, on the Embankment if he has not.

He has an easy philosophy: "All the things in the world belong to all the men in the world," is his outspoken creed, so he steals when he can, and begs when he cannot steal.

But think of this life when women share it, and children are born into it, and lads and lassies are on the tramp. Dare we think of it? We dare not! If we did, it would not be tolerated for a day. Neither dare I write about it, for there are many things that cannot be written. So I leave imagination to supply what words must not convey.

But it is all so pitiful, it is too much for me, for sometimes I feel that I am living with them, tramping with them, sleeping with them, eating with them; I am become as one of them. I feel the horror, yet I do not realise the charms.

I am an Englishman! I love liberty! I must be free, or die! I want to order my own life, to control my own actions, to run on my own lines; I would that all men should have similar rights. But, alas 1 it cannot be—civilisation claims and enchains us; we have to submit to its discipline, and it is well that it should be so. We do not, cannot live to ourselves, and for ourselves. Those days have long passed, and for ever. Orderly life and regular duties are good for us, and necessary for the well-being of the nation.

A strong robust: nation demands and requires a large amount of freedom, and this it must have, or perish! The individual man, too, requires a fair amount if he is to be a man. But we may, and we do in some things extend freedom beyond the legitimate bounds. For in a country of limited area where the bulk of the people live onerous lives, and manfully perform their duties, we allow a host of parasites to thrive and swarm.

The more this host increases, the weaker the nation becomes, and its existence may ultimately become not a sign of freedom hut a proof of national decay. For parasites thrive on weakly life, be it individual or national. So while we have a profound pity for the nomads, let us express it with a strong hand. They cannot care for themselves in any decent way. Let us care for them, and detain them in places that will allow permanent detention and segregation. And the results will be surprising, for prisons will be less numerous, workhouses, casual wards and asylums less necessary, lazar houses with their pestilential breath will pass away, and England will be happier, sweeter and more free!

"The Disappearance of Claire Newhall"

Being an Excerpt from

Chapter Seven: The Trials of Spring

of

The Consulting Detective Trilogy Part III: Montague Street

by

Darlene A. Cypser

[May 31, 1877 - Twenty-three year old Sherlock Holmes is attempting to start his detective practice while sharing rooms with his brother Mycroft.]

It was a blustery day in London on the last day of May. The barometer was dropping, but Sherlock Holmes' temper was up. He was pacing the floor of the sitting room in Montague Street.

"Sit down, Sherlock," Mycroft said without looking up from *The Times*. "You are making me dizzy."

He sat down.

"How could my pacing be making you dizzy when you weren't even looking at me?" Sherlock asked his brother.

"The sound of your footsteps was tiring," Mycroft countered.

"You are changing the facts. A sound alone cannot make you dizzy," Sherlock scoffed.

"I will concede the point. But don't you have something better to do than wear out the rug?" Mycroft asked.

"I wish I could say I did. This city is full of crimes I could solve if given the chance," Sherlock said.

"No clients this week?"

"None."

"No responses to your letters?" Mycroft asked while turning a page of *The Times*.

"None bringing me any work to do," Sherlock said impatiently as he jumped up and resumed his pacing, mumbling more to himself than to his brother as he did.

"No interesting cases at the Old Bailey?"

"No. There are plenty of crimes and criminals, but does anyone have the presence of mind to look at advertisements in the newspaper when faced with trouble?" Sherlock ranted. "Perhaps not. But perhaps a friend may see it and recommend that they call? I have to reach them somehow. I know I can help if they would just let me.

"There are numerous disappearances that have never been solved. For example, on December 12, 1829, John Ten Eyck Lansing, Jr., a prominent American politician and previously Chancellor of New York, the highest judicial officer in the state, left his Manhattan hotel to mail a letter at a New York City post office and was never seen again," he continued.

"Less than four years ago on September 3, 1873, James Burne Worson bet his friends that he could run from Leamington to Coventry. The friends followed him in a cart. They told the police that a few miles along the road Worson stumbled and disappeared while they were watching, an absurd claim. Yet the case remains unsolved. There are many more such unsolved disappearances because no competent detective was called in."

Sherlock picked up a section of the *Daily Telegraph* from the floor. He jabbed his finger at it as he continued talking and pacing from the fireplace and back.

"For example, this case has been haunting the newspapers for three days. A young woman, Claire Newhall, is said to have vanished from her home sometime Sunday night or early Monday morning. The police initially had but one idea: an elopement. After querying nearly every young man for a mile around her home they have dismissed it as merely an unfathomable woman's whim. The newspapers report her mother does not think they are looking any more. After three days they have given up!"

Sherlock sat down, dropped the newspaper, and buried his head in his hands.

"Sherlock," Mycroft said.

Silence.

"Sherlock. Stop. Either solve the case or stop following it before it tears you apart."

Without a word Sherlock Holmes pulled in his boots, tossed aside his dressing gown, grabbed his hat and coat, and left. He passed the housekeeper at the door as he went out.

"Well, where is he off to in such a rush?" Mrs Denton asked.

"To find a young woman, I suppose."

"About time. You should find one for yourself."

Mycroft laughed, but didn't bother to correct her.

"But for now all you have is me. Would you like your tea, Mr Mycroft?"

Claire Newhall lived with her mother in some rooms at Furnival Inn, Holborn. The building had once been one of the Inns of Court. It had been sold and converted to flats decades ago while retaining "inn" in the name. It was said that Charles Dickens had lived there in his bachelor days. It was but a short walk from Montague Street.

As Sherlock Holmes approached the building he noticed a number of loungers about, members of the press most likely. A bobby stood at the entrance. Holmes paused, took out his pocket book, tore a page out, and wrote a note. He approached the entrance.

"Just move along," the bobby said.

"Good day, constable," Holmes said tipping his hat. "You mistake me for a member of the press. I merely seek to deliver this note to Mrs Newhall. I am a detective and I think I can assist her. Here is my card."

He held out the note and his card.

"Whot's this?" the man said taking them from his hands.

"You are welcome to read them."

He squinted at them both and back at Sherlock Holmes.

"Aw right, go ahead," the constable said handing them back. "Y'know the number?"

Holmes said he did. He proceeded to it and knocked on the door. A small grey-haired woman opened the door. She looked hopefully up at him with red-rimmed eyes.

"Pardon me, madam. My name is Sherlock Holmes. I come in the hopes that I might be a service. I have written down some of my accomplishments in similar matters by way of introduction."

She took the note and his card.

"You did these things that you wrote?" she asked after a moment.

"I did indeed, ma'am. You may check with Inspector Gregson."

"Come in then and have a seat, young man."

He followed her inside and sat.

"Mrs Newhall, I would like to find your daughter. I have read what the papers say but they leave many questions. May I ask you?"

"I will tell you everything I know."

"Do you think anyone would kidnap your daughter for ransom?

"Good heavens, no. I don't have any money."

"No wealthy relatives?"

"No."

"Have you had any disagreements with her recently?"

"Not really."

"You hesitate. Tell me."

"Well, I felt she should find herself a husband. There were several eligible men about. We live so close to the Inns that there are a number of barristers and solicitors to be seen in the neighbourhood. She said they were all too old. So I arranged an introduction to the son of a barrister, nephew of a friend of mine. We had him over to tea once. He is studying at the University of London, a very nice young man. She was not interested. There are also medical students hereabouts studying at that University of London and at St Bartholomew's Hospital. I even suggested the greengrocer's son."

"She was not interested in any of them?"

"No. I am afraid I might have upset her by urging them on her."

"Do you think she ran away because she was angry with you?"

"That would not be like Claire at all. I don't think she was really angry. I think she just felt pestered."

"May I see her room?"

"Of course, if you think it might be helpful."

Claire's room was sparsely decorated. There was a photograph of a man in uniform.

"That is her father," Mrs Newhall said. "He's been gone many years."

There were a few photographs of girls with nuns.

"Where were these taken?" Holmes asked.

"The convent school of St Etheldreda in Ely Place."

"In Holburn?"

"Yes. Not far from here."

"Which one is your daughter?"

"That's her," she said pointing to one of the girls. "That was taken about five years ago."

"Do you have a recent picture of Claire?"

"Yes. I will get one for you."

When she left the room, Holmes looked about it. Once again he noticed how sparse it was. There was a small writing desk with some paper and pens and the photographs. He picked up a piece of writing paper and held it up to the light. He could not see any impressions. There was a book about the history of Norfolk and a few religious tracts stacked neatly. It was all so orderly, except the bed. The counterpane and blankets were in a heap. He examined the window. It was latched. The outer sill was a mere three inches. The inner and outer sills were clean.

Claire's mother returned.

"Here. This was a taken a few months ago."

Sherlock Holmes took the photograph and placed it in his pocket book.

"Is the bed the way you found it?"

"Yes, and that is highly unusual. She always made her bed when she rose."

"But nothing was knocked about in here?"

"No. The door was open and the front door of the flat was standing open."

"So it is like she sat up in bed, walked out the door, and disappeared."

"Yes."

"Are her shoes all here?"

"I hadn't thought of that and the police didn't ask."

She looked in the closet.

"Yes. How strange."

"And her slippers?"

"Yes. They are here, too. How very, very strange that she would walk out in her bare feet. Mr Holmes, I think you are making the mystery darker rather than lighter!"

"Mrs Newhall, you have told me of the young men Claire was not interested in, what of those she was interested in?"

"There weren't any to my knowledge."

"Are you certain there weren't any secret admirers?"

"Well, no, I am not certain. Mr Holmes, my greatest fear is that she has run off with some soldier."

"Why would you fear that if you desired her to marry?"

"My husband was an officer with the East India Company stationed at Meerut when the Indian Mutiny broke out. We were preparing to attend church when the Sepoys broke into the civilian quarters and the officer quarters. Claire doesn't remember it, but I do. They set some buildings on fire. There was gunfire and swords everywhere. I held her close to me and ran. It was later they told me that Philip had been killed. We came back to England after that. We've lived a retiring life. Claire was educated at the convent school of St Etheldreda in Ely Place. I want the best for her. I want her to marry a husband who can provide for her. I don't want her to marry a soldier who will die and leave her alone the way I was."

Ah, mother confesses, Holmes thought.

"Did you tell this to the police?"

"No. They just assumed she eloped with some local young man. Why would she do that when she knew I would be happy for her to marry?"

"Anyone but a soldier."

"I never told her that."

"Do you think she knew it?"

"Well, no."

"Perhaps, she sensed it?"

"Perhaps, but there are not many opportunities to meet soldiers around here."

Why would she elope in her bare feet? he thought.

"Does your daughter still communicate with the young women she went to school with?"

"Yes. They visit each other and exchange letters."

Perhaps that was where she could have met someone, he thought.

"Does she keep the letters?"

"Yes. In a box in this closet."

Sherlock Holmes skimmed through the most recent letters. Her former classmates were talking about their children, the gardens, and reminiscing about school days. All innocuous topics. No mention of young men.

"Could she have gone to visit any of them?"

"The police enquired about that. She is not at any of their homes."

"Was she closer to any one of them than others?"

"Sally Worth, I think."

"Is this her address?"

"Yes."

"Now I am going to look around outside."

"Do you think there might be a clue outside?"

"There might be one or more if the police and the press have not trampled them all."

Sherlock Holmes greeted the bobby who had allowed him to pass and began his examination of the ground from the front step to the street, to the amusement of the lounging journalists before him and the policeman behind. But Holmes was used to working with an audience and not shy about it. He made an elaborate show of taking out a magnifying glass and working forward on hands and knees. There were snickers and outright laughter. As expected he found only a few fragments of bare footprints. Most had been obliterated by many other prints. He stood up at the edge of the street to sarcastic applause to which he smiled and bowed. He looked across the street and right and left. There was nothing near to hold a print.

He turned back towards the building and walked around it. He found the window to Claire Newhall's room. There was gravel next the building but there had been none on the sill. No dings in the glass or on the stonework as sign of an errant shot. No cigarette or cigar butts. If there had been any shoe prints leading away from the gravel they were gone. He returned to Mrs Newhall.

"Mrs Newhall, I have some further investigations to do but I hope to bring you word about your daughter soon," he said before leaving.

Hope. It was essential. He wasn't going to take that from her as it had been—

He said good day to the policeman at the door and the waiting members of the press. One very young scribbler ran up and asked for his name and he rewarded him with a card. Perhaps he would see a paragraph about himself in the evening papers. Surely they had nothing better to write about if they were spending their time waiting for Mrs Newhall to come out.

He walked down the street thinking. There had been no indication in her room or in the hall or on the street that Claire Newhall had been forced to leave. There was no sign that she was frightened or in a hurry. Yet there was also no sign that her departure had been planned in advance.

Even if it was a sudden inspiration why had she not put on her shoes?

Holmes still had a number of theories to explain the disappearance but none that explained that.

He visited Sally Worth. She said she did not know where Claire was.

"Did she ever speak of going away?"

"No."

"Did she ever speak of a soldier or sailor?"

"No, she never seemed interested in men."

"Did she seem unhappy?"

"Not at all. She is always a cheerful person."

"Was she angry with her mother?"

"She mentioned that her mother was urging her to marry but she just laughed about it."

It was raining when he left Sally Worth's house. Holmes hardly noticed. He was sifting through the data in his mind as he walked down the street. Thus far every question he had asked had eliminated possibilities. There seemed to be little left, which suggested he was missing something. The "inscrutability of women" was merely an excuse, not a rational explanation. There must be some reason why she left as she did—

That thought again linked in his mind to the old insolvable puzzle: the one that drove him to be a detective, to work on this case, and yet which he could not permit himself to think about. He stopped and broke off that thought. He looked about, for he had not been paying attention to the direction of his walk. There was a café on the next corner. He could dry off and light his pipe.

There was a fire lit in the café even though it was the last day of May. It expelled the damp. He sat at a table near the fire and wrapped his long fingers around the coffee cup that was brought to him. For a moment he merely felt the warmth and banished all thoughts to clear his head. After he finished the coffee, he filled his pipe and lit it.

It was a small place. It was filling as the sun sank low in the sky. The customers seemed mostly to be writers and artists discussing their art and the politics of the day. Their voices merged into a general hum that filled the room. He wondered how many came here every day to do the same thing.

He turned his thoughts back to the case and examined each piece of evidence individually from every angle. A newsboy, himself seeking a spot out of the rain, came in hawking newspapers. Holmes bought one. He leafed through the pages. There was a three-inch column on the case that offered nothing new. He went back to his examination of the facts. A young woman had walked out of her home in the night in her bare feet and disappeared.

Why? Where was she?

While the first question might resolve the second one, it was the second question that was most important. He did not know the answer to either.

It was dark out now and the rain had stopped. The buzz of conversations was becoming more of an irritant. He left the café and headed to the streets again. He had no desire to return to Montague Street. He wanted to be alone with his thoughts. He wouldn't sleep until he solved this puzzle.

While the rain had stopped, the streets were still wet. This brought to mind a new question.

What had the weather been like the night Claire Newhall had disappeared?

He was near Kings Cross station. He asked at the ticket window if the man remembered what the weather had been like Sunday night.

"Shore do. Twas clear and warm. Few clouds now and then across the full moon but not much to speak of."

"The moon was full?"

"Yes, sir."

"Thank you very much."

The weather was clear and the moon was full. Was that significant? Claire's window faced west. Did that matter?

He stopped under a gaslight to light his pipe again. He walked, and smoked, and thought. Now and then a bobby gave him a curious look but did not approach because he seemed harmless enough.

It was after three in the morning near the steps of St Paul's Cathedral when he grasped the missing clue. It was nothing or nearly so. He had taken his mind back to his tour of Claire Newhall's room. It was sparsely furnished, sparsely decorated, like a cell. Not a gaol cell, but a monk's cell or a nun's.

The eastern sky was already starting to lighten with the approaching dawn. The rain from the night before had turned to fog. He made his way through that fog back to Holburn to Ely Place to the Roman Catholic Church of St Etheldreda. As he approached he heard voices celebrating the Matins. He waited outside. As the nuns and novitiates filed past him he softly called out her name and Claire Newhall turned and looked at him. He did not approach her and she continued on. He knew now the where, if not the why.

Sherlock Holmes spoke to the parish priest and then the Mother Superior at the convent. He explained to them that Claire had been missing since Monday morning and her mother was worried about her. They would not tell him how she came there, but they spoke to Claire and she agreed to an interview with him in their presence.

He stood and introduced himself when she entered. There was an ethereal quality about her that made one wonder that her feet touched the ground. It would be advantageous if they did not since they were still bare.

"Miss Newhall, I am glad to see that you are safe. Your mother has been worried about you."

"She need not worry," she said with a ghostly smile.

"You have been missing for five days and the police have been looking for you."

"Has it been that long? I have been so full of the Spirit that I little noticed the passage of time."

"Would you mind telling me how you came to be here?"

"Not at all. I was asleep in my room and then I was surrounded by a bright light. The next morning they found me kneeling in the church."

"She came to us in the throes of religious ecstasy," the Mother Superior said. "The Holy Spirit brought her to us and it was our duty to shelter her. Our sister Claire has always been a dear child but this is a sign that God has greater plans for her."

"You do not remember walking here?" he asked Claire.

"No. Next I knew I was kneeling in the church and I felt great peace."

"You do not intend to return to your mother?"

"No. This is my place. God has called me here."

"She has joined us as an initiate. She is free to leave if she wishes. Her mother may visit. However, now, Mr Holmes, we have our duties to attend."

He left Ely Place mulling over the results of his investigation. He had read of lights or sounds falling upon someone sleeping causing somnambulism in someone susceptible. The light of the setting full moon had flooded Claire's bedroom before dawn on Monday morning. She had risen without covering her nightgown or her feet and walked the short distance between her home and St Etheldreda's, a route she knew well and a place where she had attended school and had happy memories. She awoke there and interpreted the phenomena as a religious experience.

Who was he to say it was not to her, no matter what the scientific explanation?

It was still quite early when he approached Mrs Newhall's door with the news her daughter had been found. Holmes decided to simply tell her where Claire was and leave the explanations to Claire. Then he walked back to Montague Street.

When he arrived he found his brother at the breakfast table reading the morning papers over the remains of his breakfast. Sherlock sat down, charged his pipe, and lit it. He smoked in silence.

After a few minutes Mycroft folded up his newspaper and said, "Well?"

"I found her," Sherlock said.

Mycroft fixed his brother with a piercing gaze and waited a few more minutes.

"Yet you failed to enter triumphantly proclaiming success. That leads me to believe that those three words must be qualified in some way. Is she alive?"

"Yes."

"Has she been reunited with her mother?"

"She does not want to come home."

"This interrogation is becoming painful for at least one of us," Mycroft said. "Why did she not want to come home? Had she eloped with a lover?"

"No, she joined a convent."

"Well, there certainly might be worse alternatives."

"I suppose."

"I don't think you are thinking about Claire Newhall and the convent."

"No. It is just not something I had thought of before, that someone might disappear because they did not want to be found, and not because they were wanted by the law. Do you think—"

"Sherlock, do not do this—"

Sherlock shook his head.

"No. The horse returned."

"Yes."

His pipe had gone out. Sherlock set it down and rubbed his head with his hands.

"Have the headaches come back?" Mycroft asked.

"Yes. A few weeks ago."

"It has been a long time."

"Yes. Since the play in Cambridge."

"You need to keep busy."

"I know. I thought this case would help. I was culpably slow."

"You were faster than the police."

Sherlock snorted.

"It took you less than a day!" Mycroft insisted.

"I should have seen it all when I walked into her room. All the clues were there."

"You were not thinking solely of the case."

Sherlock sighed.

"That is true. I found parallels when there really were none. My thoughts kept straying."

"You know what happens if you go on this way. You must find something to keep your mind busy. If the cases are not coming, then find something else to do."

Sherlock Holmes could not deny the truth of brother Mycroft's advice. It was a conclusion he had come to himself some time ago. Yet he needed reminding. Shakespeare's words came to him:

What fates impose, that men must needs abide;
It boots not to resist both wind and tide.

About the Authors

(in alphabetical order)

Alexander E. Braun began his career in the late 1960s, producing *Brave New Era,* a syndicated science column, read in seven languages; it earned him an Award of Merit from the IV International Seminar of Scientific Journalism. In 1977, at the Spanish government's invitation, he represented the U.S. at the II Ibero-American Congress of Scientific Journalism. Braun joined the staff of *Microwave Systems News*, a monthly magazine, contributing to its sister publication, *Defense Electronics*. Ultimately, under his leadership as *Microwave Systems News'* editor in chief, the magazine received the Award of Excellence, Complete Periodicals Category, from the Society for Technical Communication. After a stint in Silicon Valley public relations, representing high-technology companies, Braun became West Coast Editor for the *Microwave Journal, Journal of Electronic Defense,* and *Telecommunications*. He has written countless articles, and his work has appeared in reference works such as *Newton's Telecom Dictionary, PC-Based Voice Processing*, and is quoted in engineering texts. For over two decades, he has led **The Hounds of the Internet**, a scion society of the Baker Street Irregulars with an international membership of 200+ Sherlockians and Holmesians. He is the author of the Sherlock Holmes pastiche, ***The Adventure of the Maiden Voyage: Sherlock Holmes and the RMS Titanic,*** and regularly gives presentations about Holmes, His Life and Times.

Lauren Cercone is a member of **The Tea Brokers of Mincing Lane,** the **Sherlockians of Baltimore,** the **Crewe of the Bark Lone Star,** and **The Six Napoleons of Baltimore**. She founded **The Transfixed Correspondence of Phoenix** in 2015. She lives in Bear, Delaware with her husband and three cats, none of whom are interested in things Sherlockian.

Linda Crohn is a retired lawyer. She now has more time to pursue her love of everything Sherlockian, including writing articles about the Canon. When she was 15, she fell in love with Sherlock Holmes watching Basil Rathbone. It took many years for her to finally read STUD, SIGN and the 56 stories and many more years to read *The Hound of the Baskervilles* and *Valley of Fear.* Currently, with Jon Shimberg, she is the Co-Chief Steward of the Chicago scion, **Torists International SS**.

Larry Feldman is a retired teacher living in Denver, CO. He has read and collected Sherlock Holmes related stories and articles since the 1970s. He has been an active member of **Doctor Watson's Neglected Patients (DWNP)** since 1989, having been Staff Surgeon and Editor of the Medical Bulletin in the past. He leads The Outpatients, a monthly discussion group for DWNP of Canonical Sherlock Holmes stories. The Outpatients take a member composed quiz on the target story at each meeting as part of the fun.

Jeff Fladung has been interested is Sherlock Holmes most of his life and finds Sherlock in some of his other pursuits such as archaeology and scouting. It was the founder of scouting, Lord Baden-Powel, and his references to Sherlock Holmes that lead to the idea of reviving Sherlock references into the local troop. Where Sherlock Holmes really makes an impression is in the 36 years of being in search and rescue looking for lost people. Jeff is currently Staff Surgeon of **Dr. Watson's Neglected Patients,** the Denver-based scion society. Jeff currently resides in Colorado Springs, Colorado.

Thomas Holmes (1846-1918) was a police-court missionary, criminologist and philanthropist.

Karen Murdock is a prolific Sherlockian essayist, having published over a hundred articles on a wide variety of topics. She is also a Starrettian and the editor of ***Sherlock Alive: Sherlockian Excerpts from VS's Books Alive Column*** in *The Chicago Tribune 1942-1967.* She is an active member of **The Norwegian Explorers** and **The Hounds of the Internet**. A retired geography teacher, she lives near the lovely gorge of the Mississippi River in Minneapolis.

Todd Sciore is a banker in New Jersey by day and a numismatic collector, researcher, and author by night. He has had numerous features published in *The Numismatist* (the official publication of the American Numismatic Association) where his writing won two second place Catherine Sheehan Literary Awards for U.S. Paper Money Studies. He has also had articles appear in *Coin World* and *South Florida Opulence* magazines. He is a long-time reader of both the original Canon and modern Holmesian pastiches and bears the nom of Professor Moriarty with the **The Fourth Garrideb - Numismatics of Sherlock Holmes** scion. This is his first attempt at writing fiction.

Jonathan Shimberg is a Sherlockian by both geographic upbringing and marriage. He grew up in Pound Ridge, New York, down the road from the Baring-Goulds. More realistically, he married a Sherlockian and has been dragged into this world, now being the Co-Chief Steward of **Torist International S.S.** and a member of numerous other Midwest scions. He practiced law – family law – for 50 years, finally retiring on Thanksgiving Day, 2021. In their free time, Linda and Jon are organizing "And It Is Always 1895," a conference honoring Vincent Starrett being held October 23-25, 2026.

Scott Tate resides in the San Luis Valley of southern Colorado. A wide-ranging reader since childhood, he stumbled into an appreciation of Sherlock Holmes at a young age and has occasionally contributed to Sherlockian scholarship. In another field, he is a frequent contributor to *World Watch One*, an irregular publication devoted to Buckaroo Banzai.

MURDEROUS
ATTACK
UPON
SHERLOCK
HOLMES
HOWARD ELCOCK

About the Editor

Darlene Cypser is an omnivorous reader who read books in the children's section of the public library in downtown Poughkeepsie, New York, from left to right and graduated to the adult section when she had read them all. After a branch library was opened in her neighborhood of Red Oaks Mill, she could walk to the library for more. It was there what she read through the entire Sherlock Holmes Canon and was handed a copy of William S. Baring-Gould's *Sherlock Holmes of Baker Street* which introduced her to "The Game" and the Baker Street Irregulars. She wrote to Dr. Julian Wolff who kindly explained that BSI was by invitation only and gave her contact information of the **Hudson Valley Sciontists.** She attended their meetings as a teenager and reunited with them in 2012.

Her first experience with publishing came when she received a children's hectograph kit for Christmas when she was about nine. She knew how one worked since she had helped her mother produce many newsletters and signs. Darlene proceeded to produce one issue of a neighborhood newsletter. She edited a number of newsletters thereafter, including one for St. Martin de Porres Catholic School in Poughkeepsie, NY, *Reflections* for the Lowbrow Astronomers of Ann Arbor, Michigan, and a newsletter for the University of Oklahoma law school in Norman Oklahoma. In the late 1980s she wrote and published the *Writer's Pocket Tax Guide* which lead to the birth of her publishing company, Foolscap & Quill. While working on a master's in history she edited the University of Colorado Denver's *Historical Studies Journal* in 2015 and 2016.

In 2005 she joined **Dr. Watson's Neglected Patient**s. From 2007 to 2015 Darlene was editor of the *Medical Bulletin* of Dr. Watson's Neglect Patients. She was the Chief Surgeon of DWNP from 2012 to 2023. She joined **The Hounds of the Internet** decades ago.

Darlene has written four novels covering the life and development of Sherlock Holmes from 1871 when he was seventeen years old until he met Dr. John H. Watson in 1881.

Call for Submissions

Trifles is interested in receiving submissions, though we may get swamped from time-to-time. All submissions should be related to Sherlock Holmes in some fashion. They must be your own original work. (We do not accept submissions created by AI apps.) We will consider stories, essays, limericks, puzzles, trivia, humor and art. The preferred length for stories and essays is 2700 to 5400 words, but we will consider any length.

There will be no compensation offered at this time. If the 2026 release is financially successful the initial contributors will be offered compensation based on the ratio of the page count of their contribution to all pages. Authors of all published works will receive a free copy of the issue.

Submissions should be written in standard manuscript format. Samples of the format in Word and Libre Office file formats are available on our website. https://foolscap-quill.com/trifles.html

Email submissions to submissions@foolscap-quill.com

Founders of Trifles

In addition to *Trifles* being for sale at all usual booksellers, in 2026 Founders of Trifles subscriptions are being offered for $25.00. Trifles Founders will receive a certificate designating them a Founder of Trifles, a copy of each of the four issues published in 2026, plus a 20% discount on all future subscriptions, the price of which depends upon costs of production and shipping.

Trifles will be published in paperback and ebook formats. Please indicate your preference. Checks may be mailed to Foolscap & Quill, LLC, P.O. Box 1018, Morrison, CO 80465, or you can pay with credit or debit card online at https://foolscap-quill.com/trifles.html.